How the Black Death
Gave Us the NHS

Also by Jaime Breitnauer

The Spanish Flu Epidemic and its Influence on History

How the Black Death Gave Us the NHS

A journey through the history of epidemics, and their influence on social policy and public healthcare

Jaime Breitnauer

PEN & SWORD
HISTORY

First published in Great Britain in 2022 by
Pen & Sword History
An imprint of
Pen & Sword Books Ltd
Yorkshire – Philadelphia

ISBN 978 1 39900 174 8

Typeset by Mac Style
Printed and bound in the UK by CPI Group (UK) Ltd,
Croydon, CR0 4YY.

MIX
Paper from
responsible sources
FSC
www.fsc.org   FSC® C013604

Pen & Sword Books Limited incorporates the imprints of Atlas,
Archaeology, Aviation, Discovery, Family History, Fiction, History,
Maritime, Military, Military Classics, Politics, Select, Transport,
True Crime, Air World, Frontline Publishing, Leo Cooper, Remember
When, Seaforth Publishing, The Praetorian Press, Wharncliffe
Local History, Wharncliffe Transport, Wharncliffe True Crime
and White Owl.

For a complete list of Pen & Sword titles please contact

PEN & SWORD BOOKS LIMITED
47 Church Street, Barnsley, South Yorkshire, S70 2AS, England
E-mail: enquiries@pen-and-sword.co.uk
Website: www.pen-and-sword.co.uk

Or

PEN AND SWORD BOOKS
1950 Lawrence Rd, Havertown, PA 19083, USA
E-mail: Uspen-and-sword@casematepublishers.com
Website: www.penandswordbooks.com

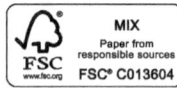

For all carers, key workers and NHS staff.

Contents

Author's Preface

At the time of writing my first book, a pandemic seemed unthinkable outside of Hollywood. For much of that period in 2018 I was living in New Zealand, on the west coast of the North Island in a truly idyllic setting. Spending my days trawling through papers and historical accounts of the horrors of 1918 seemed completely incongruous to my surroundings. There was nothing threatening or terrifying here. It was paradise.

One day, close to the completion of the book, something happened which didn't seem significant at the time, although it was certainly an experience. My husband keeps bees, and sitting in my office (little more than a garden shed in the field next to our house), I heard a noise. It was a definite and persistent hum. At first I thought it was a drone, or a distant helicopter, but it got louder and louder, and so I decided to step outside.

Putting my foot out the door I instantly knew something was different. The noise was three times louder and the energy in the air palpable. The sunlight on this midsummer day, usually bold and bleaching, was suddenly mottled and shifting. It took me a moment to realise that I was standing in a swarm of bees. Our bees. Our hive had outgrown itself and, faced with that crisis, a faction of a few thousand bees had decided to head elsewhere.

Those unfamiliar with bee keeping may have been afraid. They may have thought the bees were angry or dangerous. But in actual fact, the bees were just very focused. They had made a decision to follow another bee, a bee in charge. Whether that was our original queen, or a usurper princess, we will never know for sure, but the order had been given to leave and they were circling now, stretched across half an acre of land, moving fast but with no clear direction, calling to each other with that distinctive vibrating hum. I walked among them for a few minutes, observing the chaos, marvelling at nature. And then I went back inside and continued to work.

Perhaps an hour later, I realised it was silent outside. I stepped out again, and all was as it usually was. I could hear the breaking waves of the Tasman sea in the distance, a familiar noise that had been obscured by the swarm. I could hear the piwakawaka birds flitting around in a nearby bush. I looked down to where our hive was positioned on the seaward side of the hill, and saw a lone Manuka tree, about five metres from the hive, bending awkwardly down to one side. I walked down and saw the bees gathered on a branch together, so heavy they were pulling the whole tree over, in a tear drop bundle the size of a small Pilates ball. I looked closely and saw they were huddled, barely moving, suspended not just in the tree but in life. All activity had ceased while they considered their options. Having realised that their world had suddenly changed, they gathered together and forced each other to pause. In stillness, they waited for whatever would happen next. And then, unheard by me, a command was given and the bees were busy again, disappearing over the hill to establish a new normal, leaving their old existence behind.

Back at my desk, I found myself overwhelmed by a feeling, a combination of awe and unease, and I couldn't shake it off. I felt quite shocked by the sudden loss of our bees, and intimidated by their ability to just change when it was necessary. It was while reading Robert Webster's book *Flu Hunter* that I realised how vulnerable our world actually was to another pandemic like 1918. That the question was simply, 'when?' And I wondered, could we be as adaptable to crisis as our bees?

Two years later I began writing this book, in Bristol, UK, while we were in the middle of our own teardrop huddle. The panic of the first few weeks of March, the high energy and movement as we all suddenly realised our world was changing, had come to a sudden pause and here we were – all separate, physically, but intrinsically linked emotionally. Bundled together as a society, hanging by a thread off the branch of our own chosen tree, waiting for the signal to change. And what would society look like once that signal was given? How would we reorder, and whose direction would we follow? I had thought that by the time this book was finished I might know, but here we are in lockdown three, and many of those questions remain unanswered.

It is without doubt our world has changed irreparably. But whether that is a positive or negative remains to be seen. Suffice it to say that, while researching and writing this book, I have watched many cities, states, empires and nations rise to dominance through history, only to be brought to their knees by the burden of disease. But more often than not, something better was eventually birthed from the ruins. Humans tend to think within the boundaries of their own lifetime, but the benefit of the study of history is that bigger global picture, that development of society and societal norms across the ages, and that commitment that we all have – whether we realise it or not – to build something more sustainable for the people of the future. People we will never meet, but whose lives we ultimately have a stake in. It was this logic that led to the creation of the NHS, and it is this logic that gives us the strength to fight for its retention.

Nye Bevan, the Minister for Health who ushered in the NHS in post-war Britain, once said:

> 'Illness is neither an indulgence for which people have to pay, nor an offence for which they should be penalised, but a misfortune – the cost of which should be shared by the community.'

That has never been more evident in our lifetime than during the pandemic. If at the end of all this loss and hardship the result is a better funded, more respected and fully protected NHS, then at least we will have secured a future for our children and grandchildren that comes from a place of understanding and respect. A future I genuinely believe in.

Jaime Breitnauer, March 2021

Acknowledgments

This book absolutely would not have been written without the ongoing support of The Society of Authors. The help they provide through financial grants, professional advice and emotional scaffolding is second to none.

I would also like to thank Dr Lesel Dawson for her excellent advice, much valued friendship and listening ear.

I'd like to thank Geoffrey Rice, Emeritus Professor of History at Canterbury University, New Zealand, for the advice and support provided while writing my first book that continued to sustain me while working on my second.

The team at Pen & Sword continue to be such a great bunch of people to work with. The flexibility, advice and guidance on offer for new and returning authors is very much appreciated.

My family have been an essential source of emotional nourishment and kindness. Thank you for giving me the space to work on this project, and for listening to all my woes.

Finally, I couldn't let the acknowledgements pass without thanking the NHS themselves. You really are the white knights we all dreamed of as children. Thank you for your service and your sacrifice.

Part I

The Role of Disease in Society

Chapter I

The Development of Disease – Epidemics, Pandemics, Farming and Globalisation

'Over 10,000 years ago human beings took the decision to stop hunter gathering and to live in permanent settlements. Settlements that would over the course of time become villages towns and cities. As human behaviour changed, so has the behaviour of some of the environmental threats to human kind, the most terrifying of them being disease.'

Senior lecturer John Curran, Belfast University,
History of Pandemics podcast

In his book, *Flu Hunter: Unlocking the secrets of a virus*, a personal account of his life's work, virologist Robert Webster talks about a walk he took on the beach in 1967. He was with friend and colleague Graeme Laver on the coast of New South Wales. Webster has always been an avid walker, and met his wife Marjorie while on a tramping trip in his native New Zealand – he pulled her out of a flooded river. Having grown up on a farm, two of his three favourite things happened to be animals and the outdoors. It was only a matter of time before they converged with his third favourite thing – microbiology, and that is exactly what happened that day at the beach.

Webster and Laver noticed that, every fifteen metres or so, were dead Muttonbirds washed up on the shoreline. In 1961, Terns in South Africa had been killed in large numbers by influenza, and the two young scientists discussed if a flu virus could be the cause of the Muttonbirds demise. They approached the head of the Department of Microbiology at the Australian National University (ANU), where they were both studying and working. They needed funding, resources and permission to go to a protected reserve of islands just off the Great Barrier Reef to study their hunch. Webster famously recalls the response they got from their department head as: 'You have to be joking! Scientific expedition, my foot. More like a junket to take your friends and families on another of your outback adventures.' It seems Webster and Laver's reputation may have preceded them. 'He was largely right,' admits Webster. 'But we did not give up.'[1]

It should be noted here that, thanks to his outstanding research, Webster is now a member of both the Royal Society of New Zealand and a fellow of the Royal Society of London, and has said of this; 'I'm probably the only person who became a member of both Royal societies by putting swabs up the butt end of wildfowl', – a statement that demonstrates both his professional determination and dark Kiwi sense of humour. Back in 1967, their perseverance paid off with a substantial grant from the World Health Organisation (WHO), and ANU backtracking to also provide assistance for the expedition.

Over the next few years, Webster and Laver coordinated seven two-week field trips to three different Islands with up to twelve volunteers for each expedition from all over the globe. 'Preference was given to families with teenage children, who had the advantage of being lighter than adults and so would be less likely to break through the shallow sand burrows of the Muttonbirds and squash them.'[2] He goes on to detail the idyllic nature of the remote landscapes they were able to call home each time, and how they spent their days swimming and snorkelling around the coral reefs, catching fresh fish and lobster to eat, and then in the evenings the science would start as the birds would return to their burrows after a day of hunting for food. They would take a blood sample and a swab from the throat and cloaca, and place the samples in nitrogen cooled flasks to be studied back on the main land.

Although their accounts of these trips are full of gripping stories of being cornered by sharks, avoiding poisonous fish and a child riding a sea turtle, the real excitement happened back in the lab. When Laver, a biochemist, tested a sample from a seabird against the H2N2 virus which has been responsible for the 1957 Asian flu pandemic, he discovered a clear link. Antibodies were present in the bird, showing for the first time a relationship between human influenza and avian influenza. Their hunch had been right – the birds were dying from flu, but humans were also affected by the same virus.

On a subsequent expedition, they also found healthy birds carrying high viral loads of novel strains of flu, demonstrating they could be carriers without suffering from these diseases themselves. One of these viruses was found to be directly related to a different strain that had killed the South African Terns in 1961. Now they knew two things that would change the pathway of virus research, particularly influenza research: viral strains could mutate and infect other species, and viral strains that weren't harmful to one species could be deadly to another. This meant, theoretically at least, that a benign flu to birds had the potential to devastate the human race.

These days we assume disease is a natural part of existence, but actually history tells us something different. Disease as we know it today is in large part a consequence of our lifestyle choices – in more ways than one as we will see. At its very basic level, communicable disease at the rate and diversity we have experienced over the last 4,000 years is largely a result of our decision to stop being nomadic.

At one point in human history we were a solitary species, from each other as well as animals. Our ancestors lived in small groups, rarely coming in to contact with other groups, and only connecting with wild animals occasionally to eat them. Living in small community silos, our exposure to disease was limited. But, as John Curran, a senior lecturer at Belfast University alluded to in a recent History of Pandemics podcast, when humans decided to farm, they invited disease into their lives. 'As human behaviour changed, so has the behaviour of some of the environmental threats to human kind, the most terrifying of them being disease,' he said. And this relationship with animal diseases continued to evolve.

Our hunter gatherer ancestors were less concerned with disease. Dental problems, broken bones and parasites were their major issues. Their diet consisted of a rich variety of seasonal vegetables and berries and a small amount of meat. When, around 12,000 years ago, our human ancestors slowly stopped their hunter gatherer behaviour, and started to farm, things changed. Farming didn't happen overnight and at first, the focus was on crops. Peas and lentils were grown itinerantly, complementing the hunter-gatherer lifestyle. Wild animals like oxen started to be gathered in herds. As farming goes, it looked very different to what we do today.

Concentrated in an area called The Fertile Crescent, placed across modern-day Iraq, Jordan, Syria, Israel, Palestine, south-eastern Turkey and western Iran, farming here started with insular and genetically quite different groups of people. They all began trying different things out at the same time, from cultivating seedless figs to domesticating cats (possibly to help with vermin). This area was already a boon for wild plants and the perfect place to begin experimenting with cultivating crops like cereals.

At first, they continued to hunt for meat and collect wild fruits and vegetables. But farming was a way of settling in one location. Farming provided them with certainty, and with certainty came ingenuity. Tools for farming, tools for grinding grains, early water harvesting and irrigation techniques and the crucial invention of the wheel happened here because of agriculture. Later came other innovations in art and literature. When you aren't constantly running after your food or running away from being food, you have more time and mental energy to develop writing techniques, tell stories or record vistas in ink.

Along with the cultivation of crops came the inevitable domestication of animals. This was secondary to farming grains and vegetables, but necessary to move away completely from the unknown yield of the hunter. Goats and sheep were some of the earliest animals to be farmed around 7500 BC – and here farming means taking a group or herd of animals and protecting them against predators so you can eventually eat them or their produce (such as milk). The animals would have enjoyed some opportunity to roam, and to eat wild foods under the protective eye of the shepherd, rather than being kept in close containment with restricted movement as modern farms do today. Pigs and cattle came next, with poultry the most recent type of farming. Evidence suggests that birds were domesticated and farmed in Asia about 4,000 years ago, with the most popular farmed bird in the world, the chicken, descended from the semi-flightless Junglefowl of Thailand's tropical forests.

Excavations of skeletons from Neolithic farming sites have shown a clear, early relationship between farming and disease. Although our hunter-gatherer ancestors were still vulnerable to some disease, archaeological findings demonstrate an increased variety and frequency of illnesses, especially among children, as farming began to establish. While farming clearly has benefits to humans, otherwise we wouldn't still be doing it ten millennia later, it has come at a price. Living in close quarters with animals, and animal blood and faeces, exposed humans to new kinds of danger and new levels of risk – but it would be a long time before we understood the link.

For many centuries the theory of miasma, or that bad air from rotting organic matter caused disease, dominated medical practice. Bacteria were not discovered until 1676, and it wasn't until Louis Pasteur published his germ theory in 1861, and Robert Koch began cultivating bacteria in a lab in the 1870s, that the idea of miasma fell by the wayside. The reality that we are in fact living with a whole bunch of microorganisms that are responsible for different, specific diseases is less than 200 years old.

In 1898, Dutch microbiologist and botanist Martinus Beijernik used the Latin word for poison, 'virus', to describe a pathogen smaller than bacteria. He had successfully repeated an air filtration experiment first tried by Russian botanist Dmitry Ivanovsky on tobacco plants, that proved tobacco mosaic disease was caused by a microorganism that was too tiny to see even with a microscope. In 1901, the same filtration experiment proved that 'fowl plague', or avian flu as we now know it, was also the result of this mystery thing known as a 'virus'. But it was only when the electron microscope was invented in 1931 that we could see viruses for the first time, and study them appropriately.

Thanks to researchers like Robert Webster, we've also been able to see diseases that have crossed over to humans from the animal kingdom, called zoonotic diseases. Examples of zoonotic diseases include Lyme disease, salmonella and listeria. Some of the most dangerous infectious organisms to humans come from animals, including anthrax, Ebola and plague. Living and working with animals, especially farm animals, has resulted in the development of zoonotic diseases. But back in ancient times, with no clear link between hygiene and disease before these discoveries, there was no real concern about the risk of living in close quarters with animals.

During the Middle Ages in Europe, farming was a village-centric, collaborative affair, with villagers allocated space in surrounding fields, and common land available for grazing cattle. By this time, the natural human diet had narrowed in variety as farmers focused on crops that were easier to grow and had a higher yield. Oats, wheat and barley were the most common in Europe, foods that our stone age counterparts would not have eaten at all. The effect of monoculture crops on human health is something we will cover more in the chapter about pandemic obesity – but for now, just hold the thought in your head that a reliant food supply and healthy people don't necessary go hand in hand.

Farmers in the Middle Ages grew food for subsistence – for villagers own use, with about a fifth of their crops being given away to the Lords and Church for taxes and land rent. But by the 1500s, land had started to be bought by private investors, who began to farm for productivity and profit rather than personal reasons. Local and then regional markets began to appear in towns where people could sell the produce from their farmland. Farming had become a business, and the second agricultural revolution was under way.

The rise of modern, and later, industrial, agriculture methods had two very important knock-on effects for the progressive link between farming and disease. The first and most obvious to see is the relationship between high crop yield and livestock produce, and feeding lots of people. The population of Great Britain as we know it today had hit highs of almost 6 million people several times since the Romans' demise. But it wasn't sustainable in large part because there simply wasn't enough food for all those people. The change in farming and livestock rearing methods allowed a much higher yield of food – 6 to 12 bushels of grain crops per acre was common in the Middle Ages, but by 1850 that had risen to 23 to 30 bushels per acre.[3] More food has facilitated more people, who moved to urban centres to get industrial jobs to earn money to buy the food they no longer grew. This has resulted in the world we live in today where millions of us exist shoulder to shoulder in vast cityscapes – the perfect environment for disease to spread.

The other, perhaps less obvious, outcome is the relationship we have with animals themselves. Not only do we live in very close quarters with animals compared to our natural ancestors, but we have also experimented with animal breeding to create larger, more passive animals that can survive on cheaper foods. This has actually impacted the way diseases have changed and spread.

In Britain in the twenty-first century, it is easy to pretend we don't live in close quarters with farm animals. Unless you take a regular country walk, you may never see the living cows, pigs and sheep whose meat is common on our supermarket shelves. But this subterfuge is quite new. In London at the start of the nineteenth century, over 30,000 cattle were driven through the streets each week. In his book, *City of Beasts: How animals shaped Georgian London,* Thomas Almeroth-Williams describes how livestock was at the heart of this modern city, with cattle kept in yards and fed on the spent brewers' grain. Apparently, their milk was so thin and blueish in colour that molasses, whiting and sheep brains were added to improve the colour and texture. Smithfield meat market, established in the countryside way back in the tenth century, was by 1700 in the centre of a commercial city; a city that needed feeding in large volumes. It wasn't uncommon for barn animals to live inside the houses of some residents to avoid them being stolen, and animals were routinely slaughtered in the city's streets. During the cholera outbreak of 1849, inspectors found 3,000 pigs living in Notting Hill, three for each human resident. Outbreaks of foot-and-mouth, pleuro-pneumonia and cattle plague from the farm animals in the city were common.

When Smithfield closed in 1853, meat for Londoners began to be delivered to the city already slaughtered, and the farm animal population declined rapidly. But it remained common for city dwellers to keep birds such as chickens for eggs and meat. A practice more popular among the urban poor, these birds would again live in very close quarters with their human owners, and be slaughtered and prepared in those same quarters.

It is perhaps not a coincidence that urban farming in the UK declined around the same time as germ theory began to gain support. As hygiene and disease became clearly linked for the first time, farming and the associated slaughter of animals started to become more hidden practices across the whole of Europe. However, although less people as a percentage of population may have direct contact with farm animals today than 200 years ago, people are still exposed to the effects of keeping farm animals. We might not see animals being driven through the streets as we did in Georgian Britain, but they are ever present and close by and the resulting population growth, disease spread and disease variation are part and parcel of the risks we take to be an agricultural society.

According to a 2012 article in *The Lancet*, more than 60 per cent of human infectious diseases are caused by pathogens shared with animals. As early as the eighteenth century BC, the Babylonians recognised that 'mad dogs' could infect humans with what was probably rabies. Ideas of the 'seeds of disease' were proposed by Galen in the second century AD, and again by Ibn Sina in the eleventh century, Ibn Al-Khatib in the fourteenth century and Girolamo Fracastoro in the sixteenth century. These ideas, under-developed by today's standards, were obviously referring to what we now know as airborne pathogens. A vaccination for smallpox, now understood to be a zoonotic disease, was available from the nineteenth century in Europe, although doctors did not fully understand how it worked. In fact, in 1796, Dr Edward Jenner demonstrated that infection with the milder disease cowpox provided protection against smallpox – we now know this is because of zoonotic principles: the two diseases are related.

In 1788, a Russian military doctor infected himself with anthrax from an animal to prove it was the same disease in humans, and this was confirmed using a scientific method by Robert Koch in 1876. It was Koch himself who first conclusively proved animal diseases could infect humans when he isolated the bacteria that caused tuberculosis. German physician Rudolph Virchow coined the term zoonosis at the end of the nineteenth century, from the Greek words 'zoon', meaning animal, and 'noson', meaning disease.

At the time Robert Webster and Graeme Laver began their hypothesis about zoonotic influenza, study into zoonotic diseases was less than 100 years old, and had been interrupted by two world wars and the Great Depression. The knowledge that flu itself was a virus was less than forty years old. There was still so much to discover.

In the early 1970s, Webster and Laver decided China was the place they needed to go to study their theory that human flu could have come from birds. Both the 1957 and 1968 flu pandemics had first been detected in Southern China, and the country had a very large population of chickens, ducks and pigs – all the suspected main culprits for vectors of flu – living in very close quarters with people. In 1972, they were able to accompany a group of Australian scientists to China and hoped to get permission to sample birds and pigs. However, permission to sample the animals was not forthcoming and they came home more or less empty handed. The Chinese virologists they met, although very welcoming and cooperative, did not believe that animals were responsible for the flu pandemics and there was a lot of political sensitivity around whether these outbreaks had begun in China or Hong Kong.

On the final few days before they flew home, with the flight delayed and no itinerary in place, Webster and Laver explored the city of Shenyang where they noticed several duck farms and live poultry markets. Three years later, Webster visited Hong Kong. 'The first time I walked into a live bird market … I realised this was the place to study influenza,' he says in his book. The multi-level city markets featured a ground floor offering of live birds and fish, freshly slaughtered pigs and fresh vegetables, and clothes, furniture and other household goods on the upper levels. These live markets as a tradition date back to the sixteenth century, where in the heat of Southern China buying your meat still breathing was the only way to keep it fresh.

'Just about every aspect of those LBMs promoted the spread of influenza viruses within and between species,' says Webster. 'As well as providing conditions for the development of new virus strains. I was sure I could see viruses rampantly mixing and hybridising before my very eyes.' Cages were stacked five high, with different species sometimes kept together. Spills of water and litter moving between cages were common, and the cages were not often cleaned. An interested customer might be given the bird to check them over before purchase, and then the stall holder would slaughter, clean and de-feather them on site – with particles of blood and body fluids becoming airborne.

In the 1960s, Webster had been involved in experiments where two established flu viruses were put into a turkey, and a novel killer virus came out. He felt the set up at the live bird markets were essentially providing the same virus-hybridising conditions as they had in the lab. Subsequent studies of animals at the live bird markets showed that viruses were present in animals that were not necessarily symptomatic. These viruses were also found in wild birds globally, but Webster argued the markets offered a favourable environment for transmission to humans. This view remained, politically at least, unpopular.

It was not until a child died in Hong Kong in 1997 from a novel flu virus that had previously only been found in chickens and ducks that the link was irrefutable. The boy, aged 3, had not had any contact with poultry farms where the H5N1 bird flu had been recorded. Six months later, another seventeen people became infected with the same virus, and five of them died. Webster and his team were given permission to test animals in the bird markets where they found the virus present, and were able to use genetic sequencing to confirm it was the same. This bird flu had jumped to humans, with deadly consequences.

The study of influenza in the mid- to late twentieth century gave us the opportunity to see the clear zoonotic link. There are many diseases, viral and bacterial, that were originally zoonotic but have been part of human life for so long now, we don't see them in the same way and we just accept their presence. The acceptance of these diseases meant that many developed societies traditionally focused their efforts on how to treat diseases and epidemics, rather than how we might prevent them. But work on the flu virus has definitely changed this view. We now realise we have the power to prevent zoonotic diseases, or at least develop an early warning system, and efforts have certainly been redirected to this end.

Between 1851 and 1938, fourteen International sanitary conferences were held with a focus on how to deal with yellow fever, cholera and plague. Attendance was mostly from European nations, plus Russia and the Ottoman Empire, with the USA joining later. After this, the League of Nations set up a Health Organisation. This, and other initiatives were dissolved in 1948, and the World Health Organisation was born, with one of its roles monitoring the progress of disease, and tracking emerging diseases, globally. They started the global influenza surveillance network at the same time.

The WHO have invested in many targeted programmes for eradicating existing diseases like smallpox, and have responded to new epidemics with tracking and research initiatives. It's amazing how recent many of these programmes are. While it makes sense that the WHO's work on HIV/AIDS didn't start until 1986 (as the virus wasn't really clarified and classified until the early 1980s), the polio eradication initiative wasn't launched until 1988, the Stop TB Partnership was launched in the year 2000, and the measles initiative in 2001.

The Global Public Health Intelligence Network was launched in the mid-1990s to detect and alert authorities of emerging diseases, and managed to provide early warning of the 2009 flu pandemic, Zika, MERS and Ebola. It is part of GOARN – the Global Outbreak Alert and Response Network, created in 2000. This is a field research initiative, in which researchers from 600 global partners study potential threat diseases in animals and track emerging diseases in humans, and report back on their findings in a standardised way. This means we can identify early possible epidemics and work collectively to prevent them or reduce their impact.

Farming has been essential to the development of human civilisation, but is also responsible for amplifying for one of its greatest risks – disease. While science and politics have become partners in identifying and mitigating the risks posed by disease – especially zoonotic diseases – farming as an industry continues to be a voice of dissent. No clearer is this illustrated than in the Live Bird Markets of China. After the deadly 1997 flu outbreak in Hong Kong, recommended changes to the way LBMs worked to reduce the risk of incubating and transmitting new diseases were put in place almost immediately. In China, however, the way LBMs function has remained relatively the same. Tradition and pressure from the sector has made change slow.

In other parts of the world, agencies monitoring the development and transmission of disease have reported low uptakes of animal vaccinations among farmers who wrongly believe there is no value in vaccinating animals and birds if there is no sign of sickness among their stock. Vaccination is expensive and time consuming, and the result is pushback from farming communities. Without clear legislation in place to ensure practices that mitigate disease spreading from animals to humans are adhered to, uptake is patchy and inconsistent. And yet, essential not just to the health of people, but to the health of business.

BSE in the UK is a clear example of how farming practices created a new disease. The outbreak, identified in 1987, is believed to have been caused by scrapie, a harmless-to-humans sheep disease that managed to infect cows fed with meat and bone meal. This is not their natural diet, but a by-product of the rendering industry that provided farmers with a cheap source of feed protein. The disease developed into a bovine disease that was able to be spread to other species. Cats became ill first, and later, humans.

It's a great example of the farming industry shooting itself in the foot – although clearly this was not intentional. A cost-saving decision to use meat and bone meal as a feed for cows later resulted in offal being banned as a foodstuff, and meat and bone meal now used largely for biogas. Over the course of the outbreak 4.4 million cattle were destroyed, and there have been almost 300 cases of the human variant detected worldwide. British people aren't allowed to give blood in many other countries, British beef was banned from many international markets and farming practices irrevocably changed to prevent this situation from arising in the future.

The impact of globalisation is also clearly demonstrated by BSE. The way that people and products move around the world today is unprecedented in human history. When our ancestors began farming in The Fertile Crescent, the communities were self-reliant and had little to do with each other. Any disease they picked up from their animals would have been relatively well contained.

By the time, we get to Spanish Flu in 1918, the incredible global movement of people – a result of the Great War – resulted in the disease spreading around the world within months, infecting every known population across the entire planet – and killing 100 million of them. In the case of BSE, an emerging disease that has had its origins traced back to a farm in South East England in the late 1970s, it was able to move to other countries through exports. The vector for that disease is infected meat, the human form, vCJD cannot be transmitted between people. Meat from infected British cows was exported to numerous countries and confirmed cases of vCJD have been reported in the USA, Canada, across Europe, in Japan, the Middle East and Korea.

We are all familiar with the way the Covid-19 outbreak spread to almost every country in the world within just a few months. It wasn't formally identified until January 2020, but by mid-March most of the planet had taken extreme evasive measures, closing businesses and requiring citizens to stay at home, with martial law implemented in some regions to make sure people followed the rules. Fleets of aircraft were grounded overnight and cruise ships remain moored off the coastlines. All but essential travel, both domestically and internationally, had been banned in order to slow the spread. The way we take travel for granted, along with the way we live in such close proximity to animals, has heightened the threat of pandemic disease.

Throughout the rest of this book we will trace the impact of disease on public health policy and healthcare availability. We will look at breakouts and breakthroughs, scientific successes and equity in healthcare. But it is important to hold in our mind that our close relationship with animals, the economics of farming, and the politics of greed have been at the root of many outbreaks of dangerous new diseases, and will probably continue to be for many years to come.

Chapter II

The Pariah's Path; Compassion and Blame in Society for the Sick

'The biggest disease today is not leprosy or tuberculosis, but rather the feeling of being unwanted.'

Mother Teresa

I thought more than once about quoting Mother Teresa, who remains a divisive character even a quarter of a century after her death. Although for many people, not just Catholics, she is the epitome of selflessness and care, she had many critics. And if you read that criticism carefully, you will see it was not unfounded. Much of the money donated for her clinics was spent on spreading the word of God rather than on the hospitals and clinical supplies, and more than one medical professional commented that the actual medical care available to those seeking help via her outreach was not of the highest standard.

However, we are not here to dissect the work of a modern saint, or pick over the validity of the mission of the Catholic church. This chapter is about the way we view sickness and disease, and how that affects the way society provides for (or not) those who are victims. Whatever Mother Teresa's failings were clinically speaking, her role in fostering a sense of belonging for those who were ill with terrifying communicable diseases like leprosy was transformational, socially speaking. Her quote above is also apt for discussing the fear society often has of those who are sick, especially those caught up in pandemics.

I think my use of the word 'victims' to describe those who are ill gives away my leanings on this issue early on. Like British politician Nye Bevan who founded the NHS, I believe that people who are unwell, whether that be with a communicable disease or one fostered purely by lifestyle, deserve help and support rather than to be cast out.

Equally, I believe people who fall under the umbrella of disabled should also be offered adaptations and supported to live a life of their choosing.

In fact, when I talk about disability, I always mean disability according to the social model. For those of you who are new to that idea I will discuss it in more detail later in this chapter. Essentially, it is the concept that people aren't disabled by their physical or neuro-diversity, but by wider society's lack of support, acceptance and adaptation to the varying needs of all individuals.

The idea that those who are ill or disabled should be treated with compassion and humanity is not new, but has been largely seen as a fringe idea through history. In the past, people who were ill were often feared, people who were neuro-diverse or intellectually disabled were ridiculed, and those who were physically different were often just ignored. Even so, there are many stories dating back thousands of years that show individual and group acts of compassion. 'Jesus cleansing the leper' is one of the most striking examples for a variety of reasons, not least because it really gets to the core of why humanity loves to hate people with disease.

> A man with leprosy came to him and begged him on his knees, 'If you are willing, you can make me clean.' Jesus was indignant. He reached out his hand and touched the man. 'I am willing,' he said. 'Be clean!' Immediately the leprosy left him and he was cleansed. (Mark 1:40–42)

I remember as a child in Sunday school being taught about this passage and about the deep-rooted fear the people of the time had of leprosy. Today, we know leprosy as Hansen's disease, a bacterial infection caused by *mycobacterium leprae,* which was discovered in 1873 by Norwegian G.A. Hansen. It has been curable since 1982. We also know that although it is contagious, it is quite hard to catch. Infection usually only occurs after months or years of prolonged contact with someone who is infected, and according to UK charity The Leprosy Mission, around 95 per cent of people globally are naturally immune.

But in the early Christian period, the few hundred years immediately after Christ, leprosy was viewed quite differently. Known then as 'elephas', the disease had first been recorded in India around 600 BC, and was probably brought to the Middle East by the armies of Alexander the Great. It was untreatable and was thought (wrongly) to be highly contagious.

Those infected had to live outside of city walls or in communes, and were cut off from friends and family.

It is understandable that people were scared. Left untreated leprosy causes serious nerve damage, disfigurement, and in some serious cases the loss of extremities like fingers. It also damages the larynx making the voice of the afflicted deep and hoarse. In addition to the ravages of the infection itself, victims would have been exceptionally thin and dirty as a result of living in poverty. They probably suffered from conditions relating to malnutrition and were no doubt more susceptible to other contagious diseases. People who had suffered with the disease for a long time would have cut quite a shocking figure.

The passage in the Bible of Jesus healing the man with leprosy is radical and would have felt incredible to the people of the time – and not just because of the perceived risk of infection to Jesus. By coming to see Jesus, the man with leprosy in the passage was breaking ancient Levitical law. By touching him, Jesus was also breaking these laws. As a device to demonstrate the strength of faith, and depths of Jesus' compassion, the story is a powerful one.

But it also unwittingly lays bare the direct link made between being sick and being dirty and/or culpable as an individual. Mark writes that the man asked Jesus to 'make me clean', and then Jesus proclaimed the man as 'clean'. The fear of catching leprosy ran deeper than just being frightened of catching a disease. When Mark writes about cleanliness his words are not about healing a physical ailment, but about healing the spirit itself because leprosy wasn't really considered a medical condition at all, but a literal manifestation of being spiritually or morally unclean.

Scholars believe the modern ongoing association of leprosy with the concept of being spiritually sullied is a mistake of translation. In AD 383, the priest Jerome of Stridon translated the Bible from Hebrew in to Latin. This translation is known as the Vulgate version, and is not completely Jerome's work, but he was responsible for revising existing New Testament translations and completely translating the entire Old Testament. It became the foundation translation for many later projects, and continues to be the official Latin version still used by the Catholic Church today. A word that appeared in the Hebrew version of the Old Testament, ṣāraʿat, refers to ritual uncleanliness. It was applied to many situations, including people with mouldy clothes, fungal infections of both humans and objects, and the state of spiritual uncleanliness according to Levitical laws brought on by actions such as touching a dead body or a woman menstruating. People or objects that were ṣāra'at had to undergo a period of cleansing before they could be involved in sacred ordinances. People with physical ailments, such as pustules or acne, were also considered to have or be ṣāra'at. It was a word for a blemish, both of the literal sense and the spiritual, and only a priest could declare when it was healed.

Jerome translated this word as 'leprosy' in both the Old and New Testament. However, for most of the Old Testament period, Hansen's disease was not present in the Middle East. The 'leprosy' of the Old Testament specifically means ṣāra'at, but in the New Testament it becomes confused with Hansen's disease or elephas which had now been introduced to the region. The same word is used for both the spiritual condition according to Levitical law, and the physical illness. While it is true that those with leprosy would have been considered ṣāra'at, it is not true that ṣāra'at only refers to leprosy. Yet, in the minds of people exposed to the Vulgate Bible from the 4th Century AD on, the two different things became intertwined and Leprosy was seen as sickness of the soul so great that its physical manifestation could not be cured – a curse from God himself, curable only by God himself. Something so bad was believed to be a punishment brought on by the actions of the afflicted. Surely, they only had themselves to blame for such a thing?

The association of the medical condition of leprosy as synonymous with the morally unclean is still held by many today. Even after the discovery of antibiotics, this perception of leprosy has persisted – and it was this concept that sufferers were in some way to blame, that their condition was a punishment, that Mother Teresa continued to fight against until she died in 1997. Much of the work undertaken by leprosy charities today is around education, so that people with the disease can be supported to recover and live full lives, rather than cast out on the basis they are in some way cursed.

Today it is considered highly unlikely that the 'leper' in Mark was really a man with Hansen's disease. It is more likely he was afflicted with ṣāra'at in its original meaning and Jesus healed his spirit of its unclean state, rather than removing an infection. But this religious notion that if you are sick it must be a punishment from God spilled over into social narrative with relative ease, and began to be applied to all maladies, not just leprosy.

In his 1982 book *A Short History of Medicine*, Erwin Ackerknecht says, 'Christianity originally held its own theory of disease; disease was either punishment for sins, possession by the devil or the result of Witchcraft.'[1] Although during the Greco-Roman period the more natural causes of disease occupied the well-known names in medical history, such as Hippocrates and Galen, by the early Middle Ages in Europe things had changed. As the church gained power, so the relationship between sickness and sin became more compounded in society.

Writing in the Journal of the History of Medicine and Allied Science in 1986, Jerome Kroll and Bernard Bachrach acknowledged the idea that God was in control of illness – and who suffered from it.

> In the Middle Ages there was a general consensus that God was responsible for everything, including the occurrence of disease. Certainly, God could use natural causes of illness as the mechanism for meting out rewards, punishments and trials.[2]

Their work argues that the application of the notion that disease was a curse bestowed upon the ungodly was not universal, but rather applied mostly when the author of the works they looked at wanted to 'castigate an enemy or immoral person'. However, they still clearly illustrate that society understood illness had natural causes, but the concept of God as an omnipotent being in control of man's fate furthered the association between low morality and affliction. If you weren't good as prescribed by the Church, then God might cast disease in the path of the sinner – or at least not go out of His way to prevent it.

The Church in that period certainly profited from this idea, encouraging people to place their trust in prayer and saints rather than medical professionals to remedy maladies – with prayers led by a priest for the sick or recently deceased often coming at a cost to the family. In fact, if you were ill in Britain in the Middle Ages, you were unlikely to see a doctor at all. A local wise woman or an alchemist might provide medicinal herbs or potions for things like pain relief while the barber would pull out teeth and set broken bones. The priest was for spiritual healing as a gateway to physical healing, and monasteries were the home of clinical texts left over from the Empires of Greece and Rome. Medicine and faith were intrinsically linked in the psyche of the period.

The theory of the four humours continued to dominate alongside Galen's inaccurate anatomy, with little room for progress in Europe due to the religious ban on dissecting the dead. The position of the planets and the moon was also thought to influence fluids in the body, with early astrological charts dictating when and what type of treatment might be offered. Suffering was accepted as part of the human condition, and cures were at the hands of God alone – man himself could not affect another's destiny.[3]

This period of regressive medical practice lasted a long time. In a 2020 paper published in the Journal of Religion and Health,[4] Małgorzata Krzysztofik notes that our default view of medicine and disease as being rooted in the natural world is a relatively recent phenomenon. It wasn't until the eighteenth-century Renaissance in Europe that we began to move on from superstition and intuitive beliefs and toward the medical practices we have confidence in today.

However, the unquestionable importance of the Church in the Middle Ages resulted in entrenched beliefs about disease being controlled by the will of God that continued to underpin notions of who deserved help into the nineteenth century, and beyond. The Poor Law Amendments of 1834, for example, placed the responsibility for poverty, and the sickness and disability that often came with it, firmly at the feet of the sufferer. The Old Poor Laws, which dated back to 1536 were not particularly sympathetic. They were introduced in response to the dissolution of the monasteries, which left many people uncared for.

Before the reformation, monasteries had been the primary source of help for those with no other means. The laws forced 'beggars and vagabonds' in to indentured service on owned land, and made communities responsible for providing for their needs. Idleness was considered, 'the mother and the root of all vices'.[5] People found 'idle' would be punished accordingly, with a stay in the stocks, or later with public flogging. However, the disabled, sick and elderly were allowed to beg in designated areas. In London, a mandatory tax paid for St Bartholomew's and St Thomas' hospitals, both of which were previously paid for by the monasteries and served the city's poor primarily. Later, Houses of Correction were introduced where those who could not find work were sent to receive shelter in exchange for labour.

The problem of what to do with the poor continued largely in the vein of blame during the Tudor period. Little was done to resolve the underlying causes of poverty. Under King Edward VI, begging was completely prohibited and the role of 'alms collector' established to collect and attribute funds. Under Elizabeth I, beggars would be branded and if caught too many times, hanged – although she did also pass the Act for the Relief of the Poor, which established a community tax that would provide for those who could not manage for themselves. By the seventeenth century, the concept of the 'deserving poor' was enshrined in law. Parish workhouses, established in the second-half of the eighteenth century, were generally occupied by this group which consisted of the very old, the very young, or the very sick.

In 1832, the Royal Commission into the Operation of the Poor Laws was established. This had been spurred on by The Swing Riots by agricultural workers in 1830, who were unhappy with the way they were treated by landowners, low wages and the introduction of machinery resulting in job losses. Much land had been removed from the poorer classes over the previous 200 years, a result of the Enclosure Acts which consolidated small tracts of land and common land into large farms under single ownership. People who had traditionally had the means to produce their own food now had to rely on others – and with wages decreasing and church tithes increasing, this significant group found themselves at huge risk.

The riots had caused widespread damage in rural areas and the government felt they needed to take action. The conclusion of the report was that the system of poor relief available under existing Poor Laws allowed employers to force down wages, causing hardship. Instead of suggesting land ownership reforms, or employment reforms, the commission recommended that being poor be made yet more undesirable, so that it would not be chosen as an option. Those who could not find employment due to age, sickness or disability had little choice but to enter the workhouse system where they would often find themselves trapped. Once again, the relationship between physical health and morality or good character was enshrined in law.

These views through history rarely differentiated between the temporarily ill, and those with long term disability. Under Levitical law, the disabled could not be part of the church because they were viewed as imperfect and therefore an affront to the perfection of God. Coupled with the fear of sickness as a curse, it isn't hard to see how the seeds of discrimination against those with physical, mental or intellectual difference began to grow. Diseases that we consider temporary today, like measles, could result in permanent disability in medieval times. Visual and hearing impairments, muscular-skeletal disablement, and mental health problems were a common side effect of illness, as well a risk for those working in certain industries.

The view of both disease and disability was inextricably linked with the concept of sin. While some people viewed it as a punishment, others saw it as purgatory on earth that would allow the sinner access to heaven sooner. Almshouses were established as places where the physically incapacitated and mentally distressed could live – and they were then obliged to pray for the person who founded the almshouse, usually a rich man. Although undoubtedly worthy and essential establishments, they once again pitched the wealthy and able as people of good character against the poor and less able as less deserving, commanding them to feel gratitude. They were not seen as people able to contribute in their own right, but rather to be pitied, and to glorify those who pitied them.

This tradition of the rich funding the care of the disabled continued into the sixteenth and seventeenth century, with the main priority of the wealthy usually to further their reputation through philanthropy – an early form of virtue signalling. Although by the eighteenth century most learned people agreed that disability was a medical problem rather than a punishment from God, the support of those with disability was still heavily reliant on the church and the concept of Christian duty. People supported the disabled as a way to save their own souls.

By the nineteenth century, in the lead up to the Poor Law reforms, a preoccupation with mental health resulted in government funded asylums, as well as those paid for by religious movements such as the Quakers – a response to the displays of wealth associated with almshouses that many found distasteful. The people who had previously been the responsibility of the Parish or family were now suddenly in state care, and by 1845 a Lunacy Commission was set up to oversee these new institutions. Although beautifully designed with rolling gardens and good facilities, the asylum symbolised a loss of hope. Being committed to an asylum was increasingly a one-way trip as the century rolled on, with less effort placed on rehabilitating patients and more emphasis on hiding them away. Disability, and especially people considered to have poor mental health, were increasingly considered a burden on civilised society.

At the start of the twentieth century, liberal welfare reforms set the stage for the arrival of the NHS in 1948. We will discuss this in more detail in chapter VIII, but one of the biggest battles that needed to be fought was the battle of public opinion. The views of the sick and disabled we had inherited from centuries of judgement pervaded – and in many ways still do today.

The concept of eugenics had been growing in popularity until the 1930s. A dangerous idea which we are no doubt all familiar with at some level, it framed people who were 'deficient' as a threat to the nation's health. 'Defects', it was felt, needed to be eliminated from society. But after the horrors of the Second World War, and the prevalence of disabled men from both wars in the mid-twentieth century, views on disability and illness began to change. As well as the development of the NHS, which saw the responsibility for those who were ill rightly placed on the collective shoulders of British society, the idea of the social model of disability also began to gain shape. In 1975, UPIAS – the Union of the Physically Impaired Against Segregation, stated that it is society that disables people by not accepting difference or adapting to it. In short, the way society is ordered caters to the physical and intellectual abilities of the majority, and unfairly isolates those in the minority. The responsibility for change – the blame, if you like – should be placed on everyone rather than the person perceived to have the ailment.

While we have embraced dramatic change in many ways, the culture of blame and the fear of the sick can still very much be seen in some parts of British society. The way in which AIDS patients have historically been treated is just one example, a quite overt example, of how we attribute responsibility for some communicable diseases on some patients. Those suffering with illness related to perceived lifestyle choices, such as smoking-related cancer, obesity-related diabetes and even dementia, which has some lifestyle indicators, have also reported feeling discriminated against.

The persistence of value judgements placed on those who are unwell was brought in to sharp focus during the Covid-19 pandemic in the UK, where contracting the SARS-COV-2 virus not only came with weighted questions about your pattern of behaviour over the previous weeks, but also made the newly diagnosed responsible for the health of others with whom they may have come into contact. Track and trace activity, while well-meaning and potentially life-saving in some circumstances, just compounded this idea of blame and responsibility. Social media allowed the average person to unofficially police the activities of those around them in both physical and digital spaces, and make snap decisions about how dangerous that behaviour was – and therefore how much blame they should carry if someone they came in to contact with became ill. Government messaging also reinforced this idea that we were all culpable. The early slogan of, 'stay at home, protect the NHS, save lives', left little room for manoeuvre. There was also an emotive series of UK government ads showing people wearing oxygen masks and making statements like, 'tell her you never bend the rules'. This messaging did not foster a nostalgic wartime spirit of 'we're all in this together', but more a fearful, McCarthy-era feeling of 'reds under the bed'. We feared not just being a victim, but being blamed for creating other victims.

The irony of laying blame for being unwell at the feet of those who have contracted – and therefore possibly spread – a communicable disease is that it actually makes it harder to fight a pandemic. An article by Vaishnavi Chandrashekhar in the magazine *Science* in September 2020 looked at how stigma and blame negatively affect the fight against contagious disease. She writes that in India, doctors avoided tests for Covid because they feared the reaction of their neighbours. Across the cities, in both poor communities and the wealthier neighbourhoods where people are usually more highly educated, the response to a positive test was strikingly similar. The isolating sick were shunned, neighbours did not offer help with things like shopping, and social media was used as a way to ridicule, or 'out', those with a positive test.

Chandrashekhar notes that the People Living with HIV Stigma Index launched in 2008 had interviewed more than 100,000 people across fifty different languages by 2017. It asked questions of people living with HIV about the stigma of the diagnosis and found that those who were HIV positive reported a significant psychological burden as a result. Fear of judgement made them less likely to seek diagnosis, to adhere to treatment, or to visit clinics. Many people with HIV did not get care until they were very ill. Other studies have shown that some people with HIV, like sex workers in Russia, had been refused medical help because of their job. There are seventy-two countries where not disclosing your HIV status to a sexual partner can be a criminal offense, including in the UK. Around thirty countries still ban people who are HIV positive from entering for visits or becoming residents, or have restrictions on travel for those with HIV positive status.

When so much stigma is attached to disease, it is no wonder that people avoid getting tested, treated, or admitting to friends and family that they have contracted it. Avoiding treatment or information sharing makes the spread of disease worse. Removing blame from people and refocusing the battle on to the disease or illness itself is the only way to move past the associated stigma. Having a healthcare system that is free at the point of use was meant to assist with that step forward, to level the playing field and make access to healthcare a universal right. But it seems there is still a moral battle to be fought within society itself, because public healthcare is only effective once the patient has chosen to receive it, and crossed the clinic's threshold.

Chapter III

Disease and the Health of Society – Epidemics from Prehistory to Antiquity

'No fear of gods or law of men restrained ... no one expected that he would live to be called to account and pay the penalty of his misdeeds.'

Thucydides, *History of the Peloponnesian War*, 404 BC

Serious disease was not unfamiliar to ancient civilisations, and diseases that affected entire geographical areas were perhaps more commonplace than the historical accounts we have of them. It is likely that there were incidences of epidemic disease that went unrecorded, or the accounts were lost to time.

By 1700 BC, the ancient Near East was comprised of a number of relatively sophisticated societies, from Egypt through the Levant to Babylon. Year-round agriculture facilitated low-level urbanisation, with city-states based around the palaces of the rich and the temples of the gods. Peasants, craftsmen and the military elite lived in strict social tiers, but despite the class separation they still lived in close quarters. Although raiders from the central Asian planes were becoming increasingly common, the different societies didn't mix all that much. But as time went on the need to trade, and the need to expand mining operations to other locations (and the search for alternative metals), resulted in much more human contact.

In 1200 BC, just 500 years from the height of what we now call the Bronze Age, all the known civilisations in the Near East collapsed suddenly and catastrophically. Over a very short period (historically speaking) of just fifty years, the Bronze Age city states were abandoned, sometimes destroyed by fire. Mass migration, natural disasters such as earthquakes, increased raids from Asia and the Mediterranean and changes in warfare are all listed as the possible collective causes of this catastrophe. There is evidence to support all of these, but the role of disease should not be underestimated.

Philip Norrie, in his 2016 book *A History of Disease in Ancient Times – More Lethal Than War*, argues that a cascade of events started with natural disasters, causing drought and famine which was aggravated by raiders, weakened the populations making them more prone to disease. Epidemic disease would certainly explain why cities were more affected than rural areas, why whole settlements were left abandoned but intact for centuries, and would explain why all sectors of society were affected. Social collapse is a common side effect of serious epidemic disease, with the loss of control that comes with the death or incapacitation of military and/or religious leaders.

Researcher J. Lawrence Angel found traces of lethal malaria strains in DNA from skeletons of that period, and Emeritus Professor of Oxford University Robert Arnott has suggested that drought linked to climate change could have led to epidemic outbreaks of cholera and typhoid. Others have posited bubonic plague and smallpox – and there is empirical archaeological evidence to support all these different ideas, but not enough to give any conclusive answers. Perhaps this is because no one disease was responsible for the collapse of these empires. Norrie himself says:

> Because of the timeframe of about fifty years from c.1200–1150 BCE there was plenty of time to have several major lethal epidemics such as bubonic plague, smallpox and tularaemia occur on a widespread scale, supported by more local epidemics such as dysentery, poliomyelitis, tuberculosis, measles, influenza, anthrax and malaria. In a time of poor hygiene, no antibiotics and no vaccines these infections ... had the potential to devastate the Near East.[1]

At the same time as civilisations in the Near East were suffering, the people of the Indus Valley in modern-day India and Pakistan were undergoing a similar ordeal. In 2014, scientists from the University of Cambridge discovered evidence in preserved snail shells of serious drought, confirming theories that the same catastrophic climate change that began the chain of events leading to disease and social collapse in the Near East, caused similar problems across the Indian subcontinent. A decline in the Summer Monsoon resulted in serious water shortages.

A 2013 study published in the journal PLoS One examined skeletal remains from the ancient urban centre of Harappa which demonstrated increased infections of diseases like tuberculosis and leprosy in line with population increase, and death or injury from violence suggested the usual social structures were collapsing – probably as a result of the fear of disease, and shortages of food and water.[2] Again, a lack of first-hand written accounts prevents us from fully understanding the interplay between the various different factors at the time.

It is perhaps for that reason that the Plague of Athens, which spanned four years from 430 BC to 426 BC, is so very famous and well-studied. The incredible first-hand accounts from the time offers us the first window of its kind into such an historical event.

Athens was a modern and sophisticated city-state, home to about 150,000 of the estimated 350,000 inhabitants of the Attica region of ancient Greece, from slaves to educated native Athenians. It was a place that attracted some of the most intelligent minds; the forward-thinking philosopher Socrates was an Athenian, while playwright Sophocles, the author of *Oedipus Rex* and *Antigone*, was also born there. Although Hippocrates, lauded today as father of medicine, was from Kos, he travelled to Athens to teach the Hippocratic method and was awarded a gold crown for his work. This was a city with a respect for knowledge, and a passion for the new.

It can also be argued that Athens is the birthplace of the concept of public healthcare. In the sixth century BC, the Athenian statesman Solon wrote new laws to make society more egalitarian. Well known for removing the burden of debt, and opening up democracy to the lower echelons of society, his laws also included reforms to welfare and health to benefit all citizens, residents, and even slaves.[3] By the time of the Plague of Athens, public physicians were routinely appointed in the city, providing free treatment to the people. Their salary was paid by the city through taxation, and much of their work was on promoting a healthy way of living as preventative medicine. The public doctors were appointed through a process of election, and so were more highly considered than their private counterparts.[4] As well as specifically 'medical' practices, art therapy, theatre, music and dance were all seen to have curative properties for body and soul and were part of the fabric of Athenian society.

However, Athens was also a city plagued by war. From the time democracy was established around 508 BC, to when Philip II of Macedonia conquered Greece in 338 BC, the longest period of constant peace was just eighteen years, sandwiched between the Greco-Persian and the Peloponnesian wars. Known as the Golden Age of Athens, this period was made possible by the formation of the Delian League, a group of Ancient Greek states united – albeit tentatively – against the common threat of the Persians.

Athens soon became the cultural and political centre of the Delian League, and this period for the city was marked by many great cultural feats, such as the building of the Temple of Athena Nike on the Acropolis, and the Parthenon along with the many statues and decorations inside. Theatre admissions were subsidised to allow poorer citizens to attend, while the pursuit of knowledge was given great status – with medicine, philosophy and history well respected. Piraeus, an important port city that belonged to Athens, meant Athenians enjoyed incredible imports such as literature from the Sumerians and sculpture from Egypt, which all fed into the city's unique culture and ethos. Plato famously said: 'What the Greeks borrow from foreigners, they perfect.'

The statesman of the era, Pericles, was known for his impressive speeches, and was friends with many of the 'big names' of Athens at that time. Democracy was important to Athenians (notwithstanding the slaves, of course), as well as individualism and openness – and there was an order to city life, a sophistication, that relied on respecting each other and respecting the gods. In her book, *Introducing the Ancient Greeks*, Edith Hall notes a line from a famous speech by Pericles in 431 BC; 'We throw open our city to the world, and never expel a foreigner or prevent him from seeing or learning anything.' Hall says, 'Athenian citizens took pride in being supreme transnational "minglers".'

Athens may have been a picture of modern, gentrified civilisation in many respects, but the other great Greek city-state of the time, and fellow Delian League member, Sparta, was quite different in nature. A great military power, austere and authoritarian, Sparta devoted its attention to one thing alone – the art of war. There are no great works of art, poems or plays from classical Sparta. There are few archaeological ruins to study, because Spartans rejected the great marble architecture of Athens for simple wooden buildings that were functional in nature. Devotion to the state was necessary, and imported luxuries were rejected.

Politically, Sparta was an oligarchy run largely by a Senate of thirty elders, overseen by two hereditary kings from two different lineages who ruled side by side. They were known as the archagetai,[5] and had cult like status among the people. This set up was unique in ancient Greece, and indeed, is quite novel through history, with only a handful of nation states ever adopting a 'diarchy' – dual ruling powers – usually for very specific reasons.

The emphasis on what was fair in Sparta was very much about conformity rather than personal desire, with the deconstruction of the value of the individual in favour of the importance of the greater good an essential belief. A good illustration of this is the way boys were treated at birth. A new baby would be inspected for fitness by the elders, and if they had any concerns they would place the baby at the foot of Mount Taygetus for days – a test to see if the baby would live or die; in practice a way of weeding out the less able, and an early form of eugenics. The value of the warrior was so intensely central to the Spartan way of life that boys would leave their family at 7 years of age to start a gruelling military training programme that would last until they were 21. Spartans relied on slaves to do the day-to-day work such as growing crops, freeing up the Spartan men to train for war, and Spartan women to train for motherhood – a great honour and duty to the state for which physical fitness was seen as essential.

The relationship between Athens and Sparta had always been strained. But by 432 BC Sparta felt the Delian League was being transformed into an Athenian Empire. Control of the wealth of the league sat in Athens, with much money from the collective pot paying for the statues, plays, buildings and other cultural accessories the city valued. Much of the way the league conducted business was dictated by Athens, who demonstrated a kind of hubris about their way of life. Sparta of course had always been different, and didn't want their society corrupted by the Athenians. They felt threatened. Wary of the power the Athenians had built for themselves, and the increasingly aggressive way Athens crushed smaller cities into submission, they demanded concessions. But these were not forthcoming.

When Athens demanded the small city of Potidaea remove their fortifications to provide them with timber and minerals, the Poteidaean's asked Sparta for help. Athens laid siege to the city of Potidaea, and around the same time, placed a trade embargo on the city of Megara – a long-time ally of Sparta.

Sparta called a meeting with their own allies, the Peloponnesian league. They argued that Athens had broken some of the terms of the treaty that had governed the fragile peace of the previous two decades. Edith Hall argues that this was, in effect, a declaration of war. In early 431 BC, the Spartans invaded Attica, and the second Peloponnesian war began – a war that would last for twenty-seven years.

War and disease often go hand in hand, and it wasn't just against the backdrop of the Peloponnesian war that Athenian Plague broke out in 430 BC, it was in many ways because of it. Speaking on the *Futuremakers* podcast about the history of pandemics, Oxford University Professor Tim Rood says it was the Athenians' unusual tactic of huddling within the city walls that was a direct catalyst for the breakout of disease. The Spartans were an incredible land army that Athens could not match. Rood says Pericles made a decision not to fight a land war, but to bring all the people of Attica into the city of Athens, and use the port of Piraeus for supplies. Apart from a few calculated skirmishes, they would effectively sit the Spartans out.

Inside the walls of Athens, Rood describes how the city had become cramped and dirty, with almost 400,000 people estimated to be present there now. Athenians lived in close quarters anyway, unable to 'social distance' in the way we have become familiar with in the twenty-first century. The new refugees from Attica were now living in makeshift homes on the edges of the city, similar to modern day slums or temporary refugee camps. Athenians spent most of their time mixing together outside, rather than in their cramped one- or two-room homes, and space in the streets and market places was now very limited. Although Athens had a well organised system for the collection of water and dealing with human waste,[6] it was struggling with three times as many city dwellers as it was designed for. 'It was particularly hospitable for the onset of plague,' explains Rood. It was through the port, Athens' lifeline, that the plague arrived and spread quickly in the newly closed-off and crowded city.

Our main account of the plague comes from historian and social commentator of the time, Thucydides. In his book, *History of the Peloponnesian War,* published when the war ended in 404 BC, he describes the plague as arriving like a lightning bolt, very suddenly from outside the city. Although there were conspiracy theories circulating around the city that the Spartans had poisoned the water supply, Thucydides states authoritatively that the disease came from Ethiopia, travelling through Egypt and Liberia and entering Athens through the port. He himself suffered, and recovered from the mystery disease, and also attended to friends who were not so lucky. He offers this quite incredible first-hand account of how Athenians experienced the disease.

> From no obvious cause, but suddenly while in good health, men were ceased first with intense heat of the head, and redness and inflammation of the eyes … The parts inside the mouth … became blood red and exhaled an unnatural and fetid breath. In the next stage sneezing and hoarseness came on. In a short time the disorder descended to the chest attended by severe coughing. When it settled in the stomach, which was upset, and vomits of bile of every kind named by physicians ensued, these also attended by great distress. In most cases ineffectual retching followed producing violent convulsions which sometimes abated directly, sometimes not until long afterwards.

He goes on to say that although people with the disease felt cold to the touch, they were burning up inside, and were covered with blisters and ulcers.

> Patients could not bear to have on them the lighted coverings or linen sheets, but wanted to be quite uncovered and would have liked best to throw themselves into cold water … Many not looked after did throw themselves into cisterns, so tormented were they by a thirst that could not be quenched. It was all the same whether they drank much or little.

We don't know for sure what this disease was. Modern medicine has identified around thirty possible pathogens that could cause some or all of these symptoms. It could have been typhoid, smallpox, measles or even Ebola. It is likely it was more than one disease, with a secondary infection responsible for some of the symptoms described. What we are sure of today is that it wasn't actual plague. The tell-tale buboes, or pustules, are not described – and the death rate would definitely have been higher. In fact, the Greek word used to describe the disease, loimós, means pestilence, and is describing the pervasive nature of the disorder, how it spread and affected people, rather than the specific characteristics of plague itself.

As well as the symptoms of the plague, Thucydides also describes the impact of plague on the society of Athens at the time. This city, which valued logic and piety, which was sophisticated and cultured, which lived under an umbrella of calm democracy and was open and welcoming to the outside world, even in times of war, was now gripped by a terrifying sense of panic. He describes how appeals to the gods were made in vain, and how even the best physicians the city had to offer could not help. They simply didn't understand the nature of the disease before them.

The people of Athens suddenly felt trapped. Outside the city walls lay war, death or enslavement. Inside the walls was a deadly disease ripping through the population at an alarming rate. There was no escape, and the usually calm demeanour of the city rapidly descended in to chaos. When the leader of the city, Pericles, and his two legitimate sons died from the plague, the impact on society was huge with many believing all hope was lost.

The first indication of this was the way proper burial practices were abandoned. The plot of *Antigone*, performed in Athens just over a decade before the plague broke out, sees our heroine forbidden to give her brother a proper burial. So deeply rooted into Athenian culture was a good send off, that it was central to the plot of a famous tragic play. In more usual times, a newly deceased body would be laid out at a relative's house and ritually bathed, while women performed a lament that is still important in Greek culture today. Spring water for purification would be placed at the door of the home for mourners to use as they left the house. The funeral would be held on the third day, with a precession taking the body to an out of town cemetery before dawn. Only the very rich could afford cremation, as there were few trees locally and wood was expensive. Funeral speeches would place great value on the honour of the deceased, and proper funeral process was essential to mourning. Annual rites would be performed at family tombs to honour their dead, with the tomb itself a demonstration of both wealth and a well-lived life. In death Athenians showed that deep sense of community that framed their society politically and socially.

After the onset of the plague, however, Thucydides describes the way in which bodies lined the streets of the city, unburied by family and friends who were fearful of going near them, and how a quick cremation with no formalities became the chosen method of disposal. He writes:

> Many had resort to the most shameless methods of burial, for lack of the necessary means and because so many deaths had already occurred in their households. They would anticipate the builders of a pyre, put their own dead on it and set it alight, or throw the corpse they were carrying on top of an already lighted pyre and leave it.

The Spartans, seeing the thick smoke from the myriad of pyres rising from the city walls, withdrew to the edges of Attica, aware that something very bad was happening inside and fearful of becoming embroiled in it.

The fact that many of the early deaths were among the community of doctors in Athens made the panic and despair among people even worse. The Greeks had one of the most well developed medical professions in early history, and although there were many herbalists, spiritual healers and charlatans who dogged the profession – generally, being a physician was well respected and good physicians were sought after.

Hippocrates had been one of the first people to believe that illness was caused by natural factors, not spiritual. He separated the practice of medicine from religion, perhaps for the first time, and established the idea that rather than a punishment or curse, disease could be cured, and even prevented, by a change in diet and environmental factors. He changed the way people dealt with the sick, moving society toward a focus on patient care.

For this reason, when the disease began to take hold in the city, physicians both public and private were first on the scene. Trained to be calm and orderly, and to uphold moral standards, they fearlessly attended the sick – without any real appreciation of the risk of becoming sick themselves. Not only was PPE a thing of the distant future, people didn't even realise it was necessary.

Greek medicine was based on the concept of four humours in the body; blood, phlegm, yellow bile and black bile. It was believed an imbalance of these humours was at the root of illness, and treatment usually involved rebalancing the humours through practices such as bleeding a patient.

There was no common concept of the idea of communicable diseases, and physicians did not seem to realise the danger direct contact with bodily fluids could put them in.

In his *History of the Peloponnesian War*, Thucydides writes, 'neither were the physicians able to cope with the disease, since they first had to treat it without knowing its nature the mortality among them was greatest, as they were the most exposed to it. Nor did any other art avail.' He also says that doctors died in the largest concentration.

Fear of this terrible disease that was killing not just the people of Athens, but their experts in medicine, shook the people of the city to their absolute core. The usual way of living, the sense of community, the focus on general health and wellbeing, all imploded. People stopped visiting loved ones and whole families died at home alone, with no one to care for them. Rood says people who caught it would become despondent and give up, while the healthy people became fearful of them. It is likely that many who could have survived, died because they received no help. The feeling seemed to be that if much lauded medical professionals were at risk, all should stay away.

While some people turned to extreme piety in the face of this tragedy, Thucydides documents another trend in the city as deaths increased – self-interest. He says, 'the catastrophe was so overwhelming that men not knowing what would happen next to them became indifferent to every rule of religion or of law.'

He describes how people decided to have fun while they could, ignoring the usual norms of Athenian life.

They [the people] resolved to get out of life the pleasures which could be had speedily, and would satisfy their lusts regarding their bodies and their wealth alike as transitory, and no one was eager to practice self-denial in prospect of what was esteemed honour, because everyone thought it was doubtful whether they would live to attain it … no fear of gods or law of men restrained, for, on the one hand seeing that all men were perishing alike they judged that piety and impiety came to the same thing, and on the other no one expected that he would live to be called to account and pay the penalty of their misdeeds.

By the time the plague had abated it is estimated around a third of the city's population had perished. With Pericles and his sons now dead, Athens fell into the leadership of a series of weaker rulers, who either served their own interest or pandered to the will of the people when it came to decisions about the war. Thucydides describes how, even though the plague had ended around 426 BC, the city was in recovery for the next decade. By 415 BC, they appeared to have regained some of their old power – but they launched a disastrous attack on Sicily, and ultimately went on to lose the Peloponnesian war.

But how did the Athenian views on medicine change as a result of this plague? And how did this go on to affect medicine in the future? Rood says that the Greeks connected disease with the degradation of society. That a healthy mind and a healthy body were directly related in their holistic approach, and so a physically healthy populous was also associated with a politically and philosophically healthy society.

Plato, born during the Peloponnesian war and at the end of the plague, wrote in his *Republic* that a well-ordered mind should be governed by reason with spirit and appetite subordinate to it, and that a well-ordered society should similarly be divided. The societal collapse, selfishness and impulsive actions governed by emotion that we see during the Plague of Athens run in complete contrary to how Plato viewed the ideal social structure. A healthy body – individually or collectively – was again linked to morality. Plato's work went on to underpin Western philosophy, becoming a major influencer during the early years of Christianity, and continued to be important through the Renaissance.

Even after losing the war, Athens continued to focus on the holistic health and happiness of its people, with philosophy, creative arts and theatre, and medicine, given high status as pursuits. The 'health' of their society seemed to become even more important after the plague and war abated.

This influence can be seen through the latter part of ancient Greek independence, and into the Greco-Roman period. When Greece fell to the Roman Empire in 146 BC, the Romans invested a lot of time and money rebuilding and financing the cities they had captured. Greek life continued largely as it had done while the Romans cherry picked aspects of Greek culture and learning to incorporate into their own way of life. Greek intellectuals were welcomed in Rome. Perhaps the most influential being Galen, who was born in Greece to a wealthy architect, and travelled the empire studying medicine before becoming personal physician to the Roman emperors. A disciple of Hippocrates, Galen's humoristic view of medicine dominated the West for over 1,300 years, and wasn't challenged until Andreas Vesalius published his work on human anatomy in 1543.

Perhaps one of the greatest gifts of this period is the term epidemic itself. Hippocrates began writing his famous treatise, *Epidemics* in 430 BC, the year the Plague of Athens broke out. Epidemic comes from the Greek word 'epidemios' which is a composite of two words; 'epi' meaning 'on' and 'demos' meaning 'people', or more specifically, the people of a country. It had been used 200 years previously by Homer, to mean indigenous. Thucydides used the word 'epidemeo' to mean to stay in your own country, versus the word 'apodemeo', to leave or travel. For Plato, writing a little later, it meant to return home.

In their 2006 paper titled, *2,500-year Evolution of the Term Epidemic*, published in the journal Emerging Infectious Diseases, authors Paul Martin and Estelle Martin-Granel note that the word epidemic was not new to Hippocrates, and had been used to mean all sort of things in the past. However, Hippocrates was the first person to associate it with disease. Unlike today, where an epidemic talks about one disease, for Hippocrates it meant the prevalence of disease – lots of different diseases – in one area. When talking about the Plague of Athens then, Hippocrates' intended meaning of the word epidemic would probably have summed up the situation perfectly. A collection of diseases in one place, at one time.

It is perhaps our narrator for that period, Thucydides, who actually provided the most important medical observation from the plague, despite not being a physician, or intending to offer any in-depth medical commentary at all. However, he notes that of those who became ill and then recovered, they never fell so ill again. What he is observing is acquired immunity, an idea so foreign to the people of the time that this note by Thucydides would probably have been overlooked by most reading his accounts in the period. Miasma – the idea that bad smells or putrid air could cause sickness, and the theory of imbalanced humours, dominated medical theory. Bacteria and viruses would not even be considered for centuries. Under the thinking of the time, there should have been no reason why once you had an illness, you would not get it so bad again. And yet, it was clearly observed and noted as a phenomena during the

Plague of Athens. As time went on, the Latin term 'immunitas', which was used for people who did not have to pay taxes, came to be used for those who had survived an illness and didn't get it again. But it was not until the tenth century that Iranian physician Al-Razi documented immunity in relation to allergies, and asthma, and proposed the first theory of immunology.

Part II

From the Black Death to the NHS

Chapter IV

The First Pandemics –
Antonine and Justinian Plague

'… later on, those who were making these trenches [graves], no longer able to keep up with the number of the dying, mounted the towers of the fortifications in Sycae [Galata], and tearing off the roofs threw the bodies there in complete disorder; and they piled them up just as each one happened to fall, and filled practically all the towers with corpses, and then covered them again with their roofs. As a result of this an evil stench pervaded the city and distressed the inhabitants still more …'

Procopius, *History of the Wars*, sixth century AD

Between AD 376 and 476, the Roman Empire crumbled – or at least, the European bit did. At its height in AD 117 under Emperor Trajan, Roman territories extended as far north as Northumberland in the present-day UK, south into Africa to coastal Morocco, Liberia and Algeria, and East in to Iraq and Syria. Trajan, considered one of the 'Five Good Emperors', was generous, honest, judicious, devoted to his wife and kind to the people. He did not persecute Christians, he increased grain rations in Rome for the poor and he undertook extensive public works across the empire improving aqueducts, harbours, roads and bridges. But he had also spent most of his life as a military commander. He was proud of Rome and had huge ambitions for the Empire. He spent his tenure between AD 98 and 117 extending its scope further than any Emperor before him. Those who came after him spent their energies clinging on to these lands.

During his reign, in AD 115, Trajan had to abandon captured lands in Parthia (Persia/Iran) to spend time focusing on the Kitos war in the Judea Province and also rebellions in Babylonia. Less than fifty years later, in AD 161, a stronger Parthian Empire laid claim to lands in Armenia and Syria, and Rome dispatched forces to defend what they believed was theirs. Adoptive brothers and co-emperors Marcus Aurelius and Lucius Verus sent their legions East and came out victorious, burning the Parthian capital Ctesiphon to the ground, and committing to peace only once Parthia had agreed to hand over control of Western Mesopotamia in AD 165. But while they had won this battle, the long-term cost to the Roman Empire was great. Something other than victory came back to Rome from Mesopotamia and many scholars such as historian Rufus Fears[1] and Drs Burke and Cheston Cunha[2] believe it heralded the beginning of the end of Roman civilisation.

In his work *Methodus Medendi*, renowned Greek physician Galen described the 'plague' that returning legions were suffering from. Fever, sore throat and diarrhoea gave way to skin lesions around day nine of the sickness. The course of the illness was around three weeks for those who recovered, but many died – as many as one third of the population in some places. This disease from Mesopotamia was brand new to Europe, and with no level of acquired immunity the population of the Roman Empire was devastated. Some called it the 'Plague of Galen' after the physician who described it, although it is now more popularly recognised as the 'Antonine Plague', named after Marcus Aurelius Antonius Augustus – sole ruler after his brother Lucius Verus died in AD 169, probably from this disease. Today, we recognise it was most likely the virus smallpox.

Antonine plague ripped through the population of the Roman Empire, killing an estimated 5 to 10 million people, or about 10 per cent of the total population. Along the empire's outer borders the legions began to fall, with raiders and barbarians taking advantage of this weakness, especially at the northern border with the Germanic people. But the plague soon spread outside of the borders of the empire into northern Europe and west to Gaul. Roman troops were so beleaguered by sickness, Marcus Aurelius was eventually forced to conscript gladiators to bolster the ranks. Elsewhere he had to suspend military campaigns altogether. The machine of government also began to break down, as town councils and the courts could not meet due to people struck down. It wasn't uncommon to find abandoned farms, or sometimes whole villages whose residents had all succumbed to the worst the disease had to offer.

Antonine plague also appears to have extended further east in to China, potentially off the back of Roman trade envoys, instigating political unrest. It travelled down to the Indian Ocean, disrupting trade routes. In fact, almost the whole known world seems to have been affected. As noted in the previous chapter, the word epidemic comes from the Greek 'epi', meaning 'on', and 'demos' meaning 'people'. When a disease sweeps through a community or region, like Athenian plague, we refer to is as an epidemic. The word pandemic comes from the Greek word 'pan', meaning 'all', and 'demos' meaning 'people'; it is a disease affecting all people. In the truest sense of the word then, Antonine plague has often been referred to as the first pandemic. It is certainly the first one for which we have more than one good, first-hand, primary account. What unfolded over the next two decades was chilling indeed.

Not surprisingly, when the disease first broke out many people began to panic. Smallpox, ushered in by Rome's ambition, did not discriminate between rich and poor, but the way the people themselves treated it certainly did. Galen and other trained physicians attended to those with means, although there was little they could do except predict the outcome of the disease in the patient by noting which symptoms usually led to death, and which to recovery. The poorer classes turned to herbalists, the gods and even magicians to try to secure the best fate.

Contemporary writer Lucian of Samosata tells the story of Alexander the Paphlagonian, a Greek mystic and creator of the fraudulent Glycon cult, who claimed he could heal the sick and see in to the future. Lucian details how Antonine plague became very profitable for Alexander, with one of his verses commonly inscribed over doorways for protection. It is still unclear how accurate Lucian's account is, as he tended to combine fact and fiction readily in his work. But it demonstrates the general modus operandi of the many oracles, cults and mystics who sprang up at the time, charlatans seeking to profit off people's fear.

Pious Romans turned to their existing gods in droves. In the town of Hierapolis, a statue to Apollo, the averter of evil, was erected in an attempt to ward off the disease. Other gods and cults related to healing included the obscure, female-centric cult of Bona Dea and that of Asclepius the god of medicine. People flocked to these temples with offerings but, left disappointed, turned away from these deities, who fell into obscurity after about AD 180. Conversely, many people began to turn to the new faith of Christianity when their Roman gods could not help. Antonine plague can also be credited in supporting the popularity of Galen. It was during the outbreak that Marcus Aurelius appointed him as his personal physician. Although Galen's notes on the disease itself are relatively brief for such a largescale event, his role as the emperor's doctor secured his place as one of the most influential medical figures in history, with his works persisting as the core medical texts accepted by the church for fifteen centuries after his death.

While madness descended upon the people, Marcus Aurelius kept his head. He was known among the Senate in Rome as a true statesman, diligent about the administration of state and respectful to politicians, often yielding to the voices of the Senate even though Rome was not a democracy. His calm demeanour and view of himself as serving Rome, and not vice versa, meant the way he handled the outbreak was very forward thinking. His focus was on maintaining a sense of interdependency and community. As well as keeping the army afloat with gladiators, he also conscripted slaves to serve. He invited people from outside of the empire to move into abandoned farms and villages, keeping the populous up and the systems of community (including farming for food) going. He worked hard to fill vacancies in the political mechanisms of some of the hardest hit towns, and even subsidised funeral costs allowing the dignity of the process to be maintained, at least for the wealthy.

While Marcus Aurelius mitigated some of the impact of smallpox on the empire, damage was done during Antonine plague that resonated through the remaining 300 years of Roman rule. Aurelius' reign ended with his death in AD 180; he was considered the last of the 'Five Good Emperors'. 'Pax Romana', or period of relative stability that characterised the Roman Empire from 27 BC, also ended with the ascension of Aurelius' son, Lucius Aurelius Commodus, to the throne.

Cassius Dio, born in AD 155, was a young boy when the first wave of Antonine plague hit the Roman Empire, but nine years into Commodus' reign Dio was well into his thirties and a respected contemporary historian. A resurgence of the Antonine plague resulted in as many as 2,000 people dying per day at its height. Dio also recorded that Commodus, just 18 when he began sole rule, was not the statesman his father had been, leaving the administrative details of state to a group of favourites. His reign was characterised by political unrest, conspiracy theories and attempted coups, with his eventual assassination on New Year's Eve AD 192. By the end of his reign, he was considered a megalomaniac who compared himself to the gods. Dio described Commodus' effect on the empire as taking it 'from a kingdom of gold to one of iron and rust'. But his death wasn't the end of turmoil and decline.

The year AD 193 saw the title of emperor claimed by five different people, with Rome falling under the cloud of murder and conspiracy, followed by the seventeen-year reign of Septimus Severus, characterised by an early civil war and a series of costly military campaigns over his tenure. All the while, smallpox kept rearing its ugly head before dying down again, but it never went away. Around AD 249 another epidemic outbreak of smallpox, called the Plague of Cyprian, spread across the empire causing, by some estimates, even greater damage and death toll than during Aurelius' reign. At the time it hit, political instability was already threatening the empire, and the mass deaths, food shortages and loss of normal function of daily life further threatened the governance of Rome. Barbarian raids and peasant uprisings became more common as the state machinery began to fail.

By the time Diocletian ascended to the throne in AD 284, the empire was in crisis. Its unruly outer regions were practically uncontrollable. Diocletian decided to split the empire in two, the Western Roman Empire (which today we usually think of as the empire itself) and the Eastern Roman Empire, which we refer to as Byzantium. Ultimately, this only bought the Romans some time. Mass immigration in AD 376, the result of non-Roman people fleeing the Huns, further destabilised the state apparatus. Slowly, over the next 100 years, raiding hoards annexed parts of the empire until it was in all practical senses non-existence. Eventually, in AD 475, German barbarians took control of Rome and forced the last emperor, Romulus Augustulus, to hand over power. But across the eastern border, Byzantium stood strong.

Justinian I was one of the most powerful Byzantine emperors. Born Petrus Sabbatius in the Balkans in AD 482, shortly after the fall of the Western Roman Empire; aged 12 he left a life of poverty to live with his uncle, Justin. He travelled for a month to reach the eastern Empire's capital city of Constantinople, which was established by and named after Emperor Constantine in AD 324. A beautiful city of almost a million multicultural people on the Bosporus river, Constantinople was the world's centre of trade, culture, architecture, science and the arts at that time, just as Rome had been 400 years before. Justin, who had also left the Balkans as a peasant, had risen through the military ranks, and he paid for Sabbatius to be well-educated. Justin was named emperor of Byzantium in 518, and Sabbatius renamed himself Justinian. On his uncle's death in AD 527, Justinian inherited the Byzantine throne.

Clever, approachable and energetic, Justinian I harboured ambitious plans to restore the Western Empire. He launched bold military campaigns which briefly regained lands in Dalmatia and Italy, southern Spain, Northern Africa and the Middle East. But the pervading characterisation of Justinian's reign was not his military ambition or prowess as a statesman, but the terrifying emergence of bubonic plague. Named 'Justinian Plague' after the emperor himself, it was confirmed by researchers in 2013[3] that this was the first pandemic of Yersinia Pestis.

Recent research has identified Yersinia Pestis as originating in China, and it was no doubt spread along the Silk Road to West Asia and Africa.[4] DNA evidence has identified Yersinia Pestis in human teeth as far back as the late Bronze Age 5,000 years ago. It is an ancient, zoonotic bacteria that was spread by fleas living on infected rodents. Although the bacteria had been around for a long time, the Justinian plague was the first pandemic of Yersinia Pestis, and it would last for 300 years.

In his book *Justinian's Flea*, William Rosen describes how the black rat, Rattus rattus, was an unwilling traveller from its natural home in south west India. Although they eat almost anything, their food of choice is grain. As farming developed, and grain markets surged in importance, humans moved grain via cart, mule, ship or on foot across vast tracts of land, taking the black rat with them. By the first century AD, rats had travelled throughout Eurasia and eventually were found on every inhabited continent. These days they are rare, having been usurped by the brown rat which arrived in Europe in the 1700s. But in the sixth century AD, when Justinian came to the Byzantine throne, the black rat was a common pest.

Wherever you found humans farming, or eating farmed grain, you found Rattus rattus. In Justinian's Byzantium, archaeological evidence indicates a good volume of rats per square kilometre, especially in the more coastal areas. Historian Michael McCormick is also confident it can be assumed that the rat population was expanding.

McCormick credits this growth in some ways to the societal collapse in the West. He suggests that as the Western Roman Empire crumbled in the mid-fifth century, failure to enforce the old laws about cleanliness, rubbish and human waste also contributed to a sudden growth in the rat population of the classical Mediterranean cities. McCormick even suggests that Roman architecture may have previously prevented the spread and dispersion of rats, as modern research shows rats are unwilling to cross large paved areas. The wide, cobbled streets of classical Rome may have acted as a barrier to rats, keeping their population confined to certain spaces, and therefore regulated by food availability. After the Western Roman Empire fell apart, the cities of both central Europe and Byzantium became more densely packed with street traders and markets, and temporary buildings used by the poor.

While this explains how rats and plague ended up in Byzantium, it doesn't explain why, in the sixth century, plague suddenly became a pandemic. Yersinia Pestis lives inside a rat's bloodstream and is spread by the fleas that live on the rat drinking its blood. When an infected rat dies, fleas need to find a new host to live on. All through history humans have occasionally been bitten by an infected rat, and died from bubonic plague. But humans are not a flea's first choice for many reasons, and as human-to-human transmission of bubonic plague is almost impossible, generally infection with plague was a singular, incidental event. It did not spread or become anything more than a handful of unfortunate isolated individuals.

Historians have noted a number of natural and human factors – some quite unusual – combined in the sixth century AD to create the perfect storm, allowing the mass infection of bubonic plague during Justinian's rule.

In 536, there was an event that caused a dust cloud which persisted for almost eighteen months. Whether volcanic eruption or meteor strike, we do not know. But it led to a rapid and unexpected cooling of the climate and more rain – conditions that increase rat populations. There were also a series of earthquakes that seemed to precede serious outbreaks of plague – McCormick suggests that damaged grain silos allowed rat populations to temporarily expand due to the sudden new availability of food. The sudden explosion in the numbers of rats must have also coincided in the volume of rats infected with plague, says Rosen.

It was the sheer numbers of black rats living in Byzantium that set the scene for making the spread of plague possible. They brought it with them on their travels, and then they spread it among themselves by virtue of population volume. Infected fleas easily jumped from rat to rat in dense numbers, increasing the saturation point of infection in rat communities. An infected flea will regurgitate a highly concentrated amount of Yersinia Pestis into a new host as it feeds.[5] Rats are able to withstand huge concentrations of plague in their bloodstream, but the infected do eventually die, and if too many of them die at the same time then that creates a crisis among the fleas. They need a warm-blooded mammal to live on, and fast – and thanks to the fact rats and humans both share a love of farmed grain, there was an obvious solution for our hungry and newly homeless fleas. They jumped into the human population, little bombs laden with massive amounts of a bacteria against which the vast majority of humans had no immunity to whatsoever.

Constantinople had many people, and a policy of giving free grain and bread to citizens. Much of that grain came from Egypt. Procopius, a Palestinian legal advisor to one of Justinian's generals, watched the drama unfold. He travelled around the empire with the legions as the regent sought to win back the glory of Trajan's Rome, and noted in his *History of the Wars*, how a sickness began in the port of Pelusim on the Nile in Lower Egypt. Referring to it as a pestilence that embraced the whole world, he observed that it affected everyone regardless of status, education, cleanliness, gender, age or geography. As it moved through the empire those who thought they had escaped would find the disease circle back around, affecting them on a second or third pass through the region.

Procopius described the disease as arriving in Constantinople on the grain barges from Egypt in the spring of 542. He talks of men seeing demons or having premonitions of their own death, while others were struck so suddenly by a fever they had little time to process what was happening. He describes the lumps – the buboes – developing in the groin, armpits and by the ears of those afflicted. Coma or delirium could come next. Many died he said, through neglect, as people were afraid to tend to the victims. Some committed suicide – although it's unclear if this was intentional or a result of the delirium. But even those well cared for most likely died, and those who lived, he felt, survived as a result of 'no external cause'. That sense that there was nothing that could be done, that hopelessness, is rife in his account.

Over a four-month period, plague ravaged the city of Constantinople. Although we don't have an accurate figure for the number who died, it is thought that it could have numbered in the thousands each day at its height. Procopius isn't the only observer who records the abatement of usual funeral procedures, and that the city eventually ran out of places to bury the bodies. Bishop Gregory of Tours later recalled that six or seven bodies could be buried together due to a lack of space, as they piled up in the Basilica.[6] Procopius describes how the stench of death hung over the city of Constantinople.

Plague in Constantinople only abated after that first 100 days because of the death toll – there weren't enough humans or rats to keep the spread rate up. But by that point it had already spread across the empire, changing the fortunes of Justinian, and bedding itself in for another three centuries.

As farmers died and crops failed, crisis ensued. In fact, more than one crisis. As well as food shortages, there was a taxation shortage. Justinian had spent excessively on his campaign to conquer back the Western Empire, and was relying on tax revenues to keep the finances in check. But dead people don't pay taxes, disrupted trade routes don't yield income and a shortage of food also means a shortage of money. This impacted Justinian's extensive military campaigns.

Having already won back Roman Africa from the Vandals, to the west of Constantinople Justinian's legions were busy winning back the classical empire when plague struck. Having gained significant ground back from the Goths in the Italian peninsula, the outbreak of the Roman-Persian war in the East, coupled with the death toll among the troops from plague, meant that Justinian's forces were significantly weakened. Driven back, Justinian mounted a further, successful, offensive between 551 and 554. But although he restored his Roman map, the cost to Justinian's empire was significant. After his death in AD 565, much of that ground was lost, and arguably the empire was left vulnerable to decline through financial instability.

Despite this, Justinian I changed the rules relating to tax on land to alleviate the burden on the farming community. The old practice was that the neighbours of the deceased would pay their tax; however, with crops failing and death tolls high, Justinian relieved the agricultural community of this added financial pressure. Tax more generally was not alleviated though, and tax collection was professionalised, which was not a popular move with the people.

The medical profession in the time of Justinian was divided in to three levels, which are perhaps the polar opposite of how we might view the medical 'classes' today. While the physicians of the court, a cliquey in-crowd of aristocrats serving aristocrats, remained at the top of the pile, next in the hierarchy were the public doctors who were paid by their cities to serve the people. At the bottom were the private physicians, many of whom may not have been qualified at all. As in Athens during the time of the Athenian plague, to earn respect as a physician in the Eastern Roman Empire you had to have your skills on public display – and available for public critique. Private doctors were therefore viewed with suspicion. Galen's medical writings, based themselves on Greek humoral theory, were the set text for doctors. Available treatments included dangerous herbal 'remedies', mostly poisons, such as opium or potions made from belladonna. These would be paired with charms, amulets, objects blessed by saints, prayer and magic.

Where the actual remedies for disease fell short, the concept of care rose to the occasion. St John of Chrysostom served as the Archbishop of Constantinople from 397 until his death in 407. During that time, he founded a number of hospitals. In his 1985 book *The Birth of the Hospital in the Byzantine Empire*, Timothy Miller argues that this founding was the basis for the hospital tradition in Europe. Across the empire at that time, Christians founded hospitals as a way to win back souls for Christ, and by the time of the outbreak of plague they were common not just in modern cities like Constantinople, but beyond.

While there was no real treatment for bubonic plague until the advent of antibiotics in the twentieth century, the hospitals could provide care. For the three in seven people who would survive plague for genetic and environmental reasons, this care could have literally been the difference between life and death as friends and family may have been too afraid to help. It also served to keep victims isolated from the general populous at a time when social distancing was almost impossible. In order to support the hospital model, Justinian abolished the traditional public, or civic, physicians who traditionally provided care at a patient's home, and put them on hospital staff. For the first-time hospitals and smaller clinics were the centre of public healthcare. The hospitals themselves were seen as a centre of excellence, a place where best practice could be established and medical research carried out.

Justinian himself survived the bubonic plague and, along with others who made it through the first wave, enjoyed a level of immunity against its return. But the pestilence continued east into Persia, down into Africa, and west across Europe, changing the face of the map Justinian had been designing for Byzantine for twenty years. With a 40 per cent mortality rate, Eurasia was decimated and power lines constantly redrawn until accounts of the plague in contemporary literature rescinded around the eighth century AD.

The Vikings began moving down from the north, the Balkan people starting to segregate into distinctive states, and the Holy Roman Empire was established, all during a period where Islam was founded, permanently changing the map of the Arab kingdoms of the East and south into Africa. What was left behind, where the Romans had once been, is something starting to look a bit like Europe. And it was this Europe, established among the ashes of the Roman Empire, that would host the next major outbreak of bubonic plague.

Chapter V

Black Death – the Birth of Europe, Modern Medicine and Human Rights

'When Adam delved and Eve Span
Who was then a gentleman?' – John Ball, 1381

Around 200 years after the first plague pandemic died down, a courtier of Henry I went on a pilgrimage to Rome. It is believed the man, Rahere, had once been a musician, but was compelled to faith and life as a priest. He was a favourite of King Henry I, who was also the Duke of Normandy, the fourth son of William the Conqueror. An austere and strict ruler, he spent much time and effort on judicial and tax reforms. Henry was keen on church reform too, and had fallen out with the papacy early in his reign over who had the power to invest the clergy – the king or the Archbishop of Canterbury. It was in his later years, after the death of his son in a shipping disaster in 1120, that he became more personally involved in the church and developing his faith.

It was about this time Rahere set out for Rome. In fact, his pilgrimage may have been inspired by the death of the young prince.[1] For any man with means now choosing a pious and Godly life, Rome was an obvious place to visit. Since the first time a Bishop of Rome was referred to as 'Pope', around AD 366, Rome had been viewed as the holy land of the West. It was the place where St Peter, one of Jesus' twelve apostles and leader of the early church, had been crucified by Emperor Nero. Under Constantine I, the first true Christian Roman emperor in the early fourth century, the Bishop of Rome enjoyed greater powers and the church was able to own property for the first time.

After the fall of Rome, the papacy spent time consolidating power in what has come to be known as the 'papal states'. By the eighth century the Pope had become the de facto ruler of Byzantine land in the Italian peninsula as it was too remote to control from Constantinople. Not long after, as Byzantine control slipped away, the Duchy of Rome was established as an independent state.

In the late 700s the papacy formed an alliance with the Christian warrior king of the Franks, Charlemagne, to fight off the Lombards from the south. This relationship led to Pope Leo III crowning Charlemagne as 'emperor' of the new Holy Roman Empire on Christmas Day AD 800. This empire united lands across modern-day Italy, Germany and France and cemented the Pope's role in this important territory. Only the Pope could invest an individual to the rank of emperor. It was about this time the word 'Europe' began to be used to describe what had otherwise been called Christendom – the lands in the West where the Catholic church exerted power.

This little potted history of the Catholic Church's establishment between the eighth and tenth century AD is important to understand when considering the later impact of plague. In less than a thousand years, Christian Catholicism went from a few people meeting in back rooms around Nero's Rome, to ruling a large country of its own and exerting control over almost every world leader for 10 million square kilometres. It was not just the authority on all things related to the Christian religion, but authority over the nature of politics and society as well – including healthcare. By the time Rahere arrived, Rome's influence spread as far north as Scandinavia, as far east as Romania – where Eastern Christian Orthodoxy took over – west through Britain, Ireland, France and Spain and south into North Africa.

On his arrival in Rome, it is said that Rahere chose to visit the location of St Peter's martyrdom, a known malarial spot. He became sick with the parasite, then known as Roman Fever. He vowed that should he recover and make it home, he would start a hospital for the poor. He did get better and on his way home had a vision of Bartholomew, one of the twelve apostles, who spoke to him and told him to found a house of God in Smithfield, London. When he returned to London he sought an audience with Henry I who owned that land, and who gave him permission to go ahead with the plan. St Bartholomew's priory was founded in 1123 and consecrated in 1129.

The concept of the hospital seems to have arrived in Anglo Saxon Britain with the Normans in 1066. Lanfranc's Hospital for those with leprosy in Canterbury was established in the 1070s, although there is also some evidence of a leprosy hospital in Winchester around 1030. But St Bartholomew's seems to be a very early example of a more general hospital in England. Although there were hospitals in major cities during the Roman Empire and in Byzantium – and also as far back as ancient Greece – this was the first time a hospital was made available to the poor in Britain's biggest city. Today St Barts is one of the oldest working hospitals in the world.

Hospitals and religion have always been closely linked. As in Greek and Roman times the people visited temples for healing – both magical and herbal – in the Middle Ages people visited the church and monasteries. Prayer formed a central part of the healing process, as sin and sickness were often closely associated (see Chapter II). But monks and priests also had some medical training, and stored the medical texts of old. The Catholic Church approved of Galen, the one-time personal physician to Marcus Aurelius, and religion-sponsored healthcare was based on the Galenic model.

The Latin word 'hospitalis' simply referred to a place where 'guests' needed shelter. Sometimes, hospitals were actually alms-houses, or places for pilgrims to stay. Mostly though, they were institutions where the needy could receive care – be that a hot meal and rest, or specific medical attention. Over the next 400 years, more than 700 hospitals were founded across England. Perhaps the most well-known is the Priory of St Mary of Bethlehem – later known as Bedlam – established in 1247. It took in sick paupers who, as time went on, were most likely to be mentally rather than physically unwell, and before long this type of care became Bedlam's specialism. It had to be rebuilt in the seventeenth century and was characterised as an asylum from then on.

One of the biggest hospitals was St Leonard's in York, established in AD1137. It had high ceilings and large windows to help circulate the 'bad air' or miasma thought to cause disease. Once admitted, no medical treatment could be received until a prospective patient had confessed all their sins. Only after their soul had been healed would work start on fixing the earthly body. The hospital was destroyed during the reformation in 1539, leaving the city without a medical facility for 200 years.

Hospitals in medieval Britain were funded by a mixture of charity, donations from patrons and income from any associated land and buildings. Even during good times, securing income could be precarious.

There were often two patients to a bed and low standards of cleanliness, and the staff were made up of religious folk rather than 'professional' doctors – with prayer and ritual playing a central role in treatment. While the work of Galen was supported, further enquiry into the nature of the body, disease or the furthering of medical theory was largely prohibited by religious practices. Post-mortem dissection, for example, was completely illegal and as Galen's model of the body was based mostly on his dissection of monkeys and pigs, human anatomy and body function was not well understood by today's standards. It wasn't until Andreas Vesalius published printed books containing detailed illustrations of the human body in 1543 that Western Europe began to challenge and adapt Galen's theories. This meant that while medical treatment in the medieval period was certainly well meaning, whether someone recovered was often a matter of luck.

In the mid-summer of 1348, a seaman at Melcombe Regis, which today is called Weymouth, became unwell. We now know him to be the first recorded English victim of bubonic plague. Although there is some, very limited evidence that Yersinia Pestis made it to English shores during the first pandemic some 600 or so years before,[2] it may not have been widely spread. But, this second-time round, medieval Britain would not be so lucky.

Modern science has demonstrated this strain of plague was different to the one responsible for Justinian plague, newly evolved, and appears to have come East from Kyrgyzstan. There are graves in that region from 1338 which reference plague in their inscriptions. It spread slowly through Byzantine and into the Holy Roman Empire. Once in the Mediterranean it travelled much faster by ship, spreading out to Africa, Britain and Northern Europe.

Once it made land in Weymouth, plague is said to have travelled west at a rate of about 1.5 miles – or almost 3km – per day. Like in Byzantine, the vector would probably have been grain carts heading to market. The rats attracted to the grain would have hopped on and off the carts, perhaps mostly unseen, like they were buses. By late summer plague was reported in Bristol, by autumn it had travelled east to Oxford. By November 1348 it had hit London.

Henry Knighton, the Canon of St Mary's Abbey in Leicester for thirty-three years, was also an avid chronicler. He wrote a history of England from the Norman conquests through to 1395, the year before his own death in 1396. He included a first-hand account of what he witnessed during the plague:

> Then the grievous plague penetrated the seacoasts from Southampton, and came to Bristol, and there almost the whole strength of the town died, struck as it were by sudden death. There died at Leicester in the small parish of St Leonard more than 380, in the parish of Holy Cross more than 400; in the parish of S. Margaret of Leicester more than 700; and so in each parish a great number. Then the bishop of Lincoln gave general power to all and every priest to hear confessions, and absolve with full and entire authority except in matters of debt, in which case the dying man, if he could, should pay the debt while he lived, or others should certainly fulfil that duty from his property after his death. ... and there were small prices for everything on account of the fear of death. For there were very few who cared about riches or anything else... Sheep and cattle went wandering over fields and through crops, and there was no one to go and drive or gather them for there was such a lack of servants that no one knew what he ought to do. Wherefore many crops perished in the fields for want of someone to gather them. The Scots, hearing of the cruel pestilence of the English, believed it had come to them from the avenging hand of God, and – as it was commonly reported in England – took their oath when they wanted to swear, 'By the foul death of England.'
>
> Meanwhile the king sent proclamation that reapers and other labourers should not take more than they had been accustomed to take (in pay). But the labourers were so lifted up and obstinate that they would not listen to the king's command, but if anyone wished to have them he had to give them what they wanted, and either lose his fruit and crops, or satisfy the wishes of the workmen.
>
> After the pestilence, many buildings, great and small, fell into ruins in every city for lack of inhabitants, likewise many villages and hamlets became desolate, not a house being left in them, all having died who dwelt there; and it was probable that many such villages would never be inhabited. In the winter following there was such a want of servants in work of all kinds, that one would scarcely believe

that in times past there had been such a lack. And so all necessities became so much dearer.

– History of England by Henry Knighton,
in *Source Book of English History*, by E.K. Kendall

This plague was worse than the Plague of Justinian. Known at the time as the 'Great Pestilence', it appears to have moved faster, spread more virulently and killed more people than in Byzantine. As many as 60 per cent of the English population, estimated to have been about 6 million people at the time, perished. Beyond the savage death toll, the implications were huge.

The first phase of the Hundred Years' War, a conflict between the French House of Plantagenet and the English House of Lancaster, which had been raging at that point for a decade, was halted due to a lack of manpower. War wasn't the only industry that suffered. Knighton's observations about farm animals are particularly important, as at the time agriculture was central to British life and wool its main export. As farm hands caught the disease and died, the animals roamed the land uncared for. Crops failed or could not be harvested, markets were left empty as both merchants and patrons failed to show. Although the poor were hit hardest (it has been suggested their single-storey homes allowed fleas to fall freely from rats in the roof,) the wealthy landowners soon found their estates collapsing with no servants to see to them. By the spring of 1349, life across England had ground to a halt.

Perhaps some of the hardest hit were the clergy, as they were providing primary medical care via hospitals, churches and priories. Of course, with no antibiotics, there was no effective treatment or cure for the disease. But bloodletting, sweating, forced vomiting, and lancing of swellings were readily used. During this first eighteen-month outbreak from 1348 to 1349, the ordination register for the clergy rose sharply, suggesting a high death rate among priesthood of as much as 50 per cent. Because the vector for spreading plague is usually fleas from rats, the risk to those treating the infected should not have been that much greater than for everyone else. But new research, published in January 2018, modelled existing data from the outbreak and showed that rats alone could not have spread the disease as fast or as far as actually happened. Researchers hypothesised that human parasites were able to spread plague from infected humans directly, making the transmission faster.[3] We now also know that plague can sometimes be pneumonic – a lung infection spread through droplets in the air. This is rare, but when it happens it spreads fast and is more lethal than its bubonic version. This would certainly explain the high mortality of the carers.

Many hospitals and priories were completely overrun by Black Death. At Thornton Abbey in Lincolnshire there is evidence of a mass grave – something rarely heard of at the time in small rural communities. As with previous outbreaks of disease in history, the failure to follow the proper burial rites is a clear indication of the panic and disorder of the period. To find this at the site of a church is particularly powerful – although archaeologists were keen to point out each body was wrapped in a shroud, and placed carefully in the grave.

The sustainability of hospitals in the disaster would have faced attacks on two fronts. First, as more people died, less money would have been coming in through patronage and charitable collections. This meant the hospitals would have been struggling financially with the basics, like providing food. Second, they would have been seeing more people – not just the actively sick who needed treatment, but also those who, because of the death of their immediate family, needed to be looked after. The elderly, disabled, young children and the very poor who could not cope alone may all have found themselves in hospitals even if they were not infected. There was no other form of social care at the time.

There was another important reason people turned to the church, and that was fear of sin. The idea that sickness was due to the will or wrath of God was a common thread underpinning many of the societal beliefs of the day. How this was applied was wide ranging. While some priests may have lamented societies general sinfulness as the root cause for angering God, others considered it down to individual piety – or lack thereof – or perhaps even witchcraft. Prayer, incantations, protective amulets, charms and the confessing of sins were all important tools in the medieval medical kit for fighting plague. Obsessed as they were with the apocalypse, Christians of the fourteenth century saw the outbreak of plague as the arrival of the third horseman of the apocalypse: pestilence. With war already present in the form of the Anglo-French conflict, and a devastating famine across Europe from 1315 to 1322, thanks to unprecedented cold and high levels of rainfall, the arrival of the plague meant it was common for people to believe they were living through the end times.

Christians also turned their attention to a common whipping boy hen looking for a source of the pestilence, or someone to blame – the Jews. The Flagellants, religious zealots who whipped their own bodies in atonement for sin, had emerged in Central Europe before the plague began. Originally a practice reserved for eleventh-century Italian monks, it saw something of a revival as the pestilence made its way across the continent. Public displays of flagellation became more common, and groups of Flagellants moved from town to town, hooded but bare chested, chanting and whipping as they went. But they didn't just direct their violence toward themselves. After a rumour began that Jews may have poisoned well-water to start the pandemic, many Flagellants attacked and massacred Jewish people and as a result they started to migrate to Poland, where King Casimir III had promised they would be safe.

According to an account by contemporary observer Robert of Avesbury, around September 1349, the Flagellants arrived in London from Belgium. Carrying a 'scourge of three tails', and wearing hats anointed with the sign of the cross, they made daily appearances at places like St Paul's. But Londoners were not impressed. The Flagellants were deported and, in October that year, the Pope denounced the movement. By 1350, it had disappeared.

The winter of 1349 brought respite. The cold weather usually forced the fleas into hibernation or killed them, and although it remained virulent during the previous winter, by December 1349 infection rates had dropped off dramatically. But Black Death would make several more appearances in England in 1361, 1368, 1374 and 1381 – although subsequent outbreaks seem to affect fewer people, and those at the more vulnerable ends of the spectrum.

For those who survived, many welcomed a better way of life – particularly peasants and labourers. Less people able to work meant higher wages. More available homes meant lower rent. Land was cheap and the previously dominant open-field farming system began to be eaten away by the process of enclosure; the purchasing of land by yeomen – or free common men – created a new 'middle class' of non-gentrified landowners and locked up land in private ownership. The workers were getting their first taste of economic power, their first experience of control over their masters, and they liked it. The landed gentry did not like it one bit.

In 1351, legislation was passed to try and keep wages at pre-plague levels, and make it illegal to refuse work. Still wages continued to rise and many serfs tied to land left to work elsewhere illegally. In 1363, yet more laws were brought in to try and prevent the new, more affluent labouring class from buying and consuming luxury products. The push and pull between the traditionally affluent and the newly socially mobile was slowly working its way to a head.

In the early summer of 1381, some thirty-three years after the first outbreak of plague, John Ball stood on the green at Blackheath and offered this simple rhyming couplet.

> 'When Adam delved and Eve span,
> Who was then a gentleman?'

In his book, *Great Tales from English History*, Robert Lacey explains that everyone listening would have understood the meaning of Ball's words – that all men were created equal, and servitude was an ungodly invention. Ball was a radical cleric and yeoman and he was not happy about the way the country was being run. As well as trying to micro-manage wealth accumulation, the rekindled war with France was draining the country financially and the Crown kept introducing new taxes to pay for it. The poll tax – payable per person – in 1380 was the third in four years and Ball had had enough. Along with some of the other recognisable names of the period, such as Wat Tyler and Jack Straw, Ball sought to inspire an uprising among the new landowners, and the peasants who shared their land. And he succeeded in what came to be known as the Peasants' Revolt.

In May 1381, tax examiners seeking evaders arrived in the Essex villages of Fobbing, Corringham, and Stanford-le-Hope. But they were met with aggression, and fled. As news of this action spread, peasants and small landowners from across the county marched on London with Ball. Meanwhile, Wat Tyler gathered a crowd of 4,000 and marched on Canterbury to confront the Archbishop. Religious authority was starting to be challenged by the Lollards – an emerging group of religious reformers who believed they didn't need priests to find the path to God. Emboldened by both challenges to the authority of the church and the gentry, Ball and Tyler's protesters eventually beheaded the Archbishop and the king's treasurer.

The 14-year-old king, Richard II, rode out to meet the protesters, and listened to their demands. All men should be equal, they said, save for the king. The wealth of the Church should be divided among society. They wanted an end to serfdom, reduced taxes and to get rid of the king's officials. Lacey says that, once this idealistic list was complete, an argument broke out in which Tyler stabbed the Mayor of London, and in response the king's guard ran him through. Lucky for Tyler he had met the king at Smithfield, and St Barts was nearby – although his stay wasn't long; the king's men followed him there, dragged him out and beheaded him.

Richard II agreed to their demands and the men went home to the East of England, but elsewhere in the country, the revolt continued with farmers, craftsmen, labourers and merchants demanding freedom from serfdom, the church and taxes. The ringleaders were eventually rounded up and executed. Although Richard reneged on his agreement, some concessions were made. For example, the poll tax was abolished and the crown was very cautious about any new forms of taxation. Wages continued to rise and many landowners sold serfs their freedom. By the end of the fifteenth century Feudalism had almost disappeared and was formally abolished in 1660.

Plague died down, but it never really went away. It was endemic in major cities, with serious outbreaks every few decades. In 1563, some 200 years after the first event that came to be known retrospectively as the Black Death, there was another terrible outbreak in England with London very badly affected. By this point, the concept of quarantine was well embedded into European life. Using the Church as her mouthpiece, Queen Elizabeth I instructed households who had been in contact with plague not to visit church or leave home for several weeks after either the death or recovery of a plague patient. A blue cross was painted on the doors of affected homes. Stray animals were rounded up and destroyed and bonfires were lit every night at 7pm to try and purify the air. But by late summer, around 1,500 Londoners were dying each week. Elizabeth fled to Windsor, banning food and goods to be transported there from London and threatening to hang anyone who followed her. Although still reliant on the concept of miasma, it seems clear that Elizabeth and her advisors understood the basic underlying concept of communicable disease. In London, affected houses were boarded up and inhabitants isolated for forty days. If they died, their house was not allowed to be rented out. These measures had some effect and by the end of January 1564 the plague seems to have gone.

It was 100 years later, in 1665, that plague came back with a vengeance. The Great Plague of London, as described by Samuel Pepys in his diary, savaged the city for a year killing 7,000 people a week at its peak. A seemingly unstoppable wave of disease killed a quarter of London's population in eighteen months, and was only stopped by the Great Fire of London which destroyed 90 per cent of the city in one night.

Much of how we think of plague in popular culture today comes from that outbreak, even though it was significantly smaller than the Black Death. The red cross painted on the door of the affected, along with the words 'Lord Have Mercy Upon Us' was standard seventeenth-century practice. The body collector dragging a cart of corpses and shouting 'bring out your dead' was also from that period, as is the well-known leather beaked mask of the plague doctor. The mask housed herbs and flowers to repel the miasma, and the hat and cloak were to protect the doctor's body.

In reality, it's not thought many plague doctors wore this costume, although it became popular later in theatre and writing about the period. What is more significant is that there was a 'plague doctor' at all. This marked a huge change from 1348 when medical care was church-based.

In his book *The Swerve*, Stephan Greenblatt paints a beautiful story of an unassuming man, Poggio Bracciolini, riding through the foothills of southern Germany in the winter of 1417, on his way to a monastery. Bracciolini was a 'humanist', a group of Italians who, since the 1330s, had been hunting the lost works of antiquity, the books that had been filed away in the monasteries – of which there might only be one copy – the parchment that had been overwritten by monks with scripture, the tomes that lay partially destroyed in the most unlikely of places.

The end of Rome and the rise of the church had resulted in a hierarchy of knowledge. Only those deemed worthy – the priests and aristocracy who spoke Latin – could have knowledge. But increasingly this group wanted the knowledge back. Just the like the peasants with their taste of power standing up to King Richard II, humanists, like Bracciolini, had tasted knowledge and realised that it shouldn't be left locked away.

An accomplished Latin speaker who had already read many of the available works from antiquity, Bracciolini would have been familiar with the name Lucretius even though none of his works were yet discovered. Referenced, and even quoted, repeatedly by other authors of the time, it was a familiar name. Greenblatt imagines he would have been quite excited then, to discover a work entitled *De Rerum Natura* – on the nature of things – by this author. Bracciolini made a copy, and carried on with his work hunting old texts.

'On the nature of things' is a poem written by Lucretius toward the end of his life, about fifty years before the birth of Christ. It is based on epicurean philosophy, and describes a universe that operates according to physical principles guided by chance rather than the will of the gods. Epicureans were materialists who put their faith in the physical world, and felt that pleasure should be the chief pursuit in life. They wanted to move mankind away from the fear of gods and death. Lucretius' poem was considered a masterpiece in ancient Rome, and it inspired Virgil. But the copy Bracciolini found in the monastery in Germany was the only one left.

That copy of Lucretius never left the monastery, but Bracciolini's copy soon became well-circulated among the humanists, who were excited by such a notable discovery. Then, in 1473, a printed version was produced on one of Guttenberg's new presses, now highly popular across Europe. It achieved instant notoriety from all quarters. Lucretius' words about vibrating atoms, the void of space and the science of the material world fascinated those thirsty for new knowledge. His ideas about how the gods were present but disinterested in human affairs, and how we should live untainted with worry about them, filled the church with fury. Lucretius is clear in his belief that divine intervention just isn't a thing.

This sat awkwardly with the level of control the church had enjoyed for hundreds of years. Concerned about their souls, people had sought comfort from priests since before the fall of Rome. Now they were seeking comfort in learning and thinking for themselves, practices which were at odds with the teachings of the church at the time. The universities, first established as a training ground for the clergy by papal decree, had transformed into seats of early critical thinking, and much of that thinking was related to medicine.

As early as the late thirteenth century, students as Bologna had begun to open up bodies after death to see what was going on inside. Andreas

Vesalius studied medicine at Paris University in the early sixteenth century, where he learned the art of dissection. Although more common now, it was still taboo, and Vesalius would plunder graveyards for bodies to perfect his art. In 1543, he published his seminal work *The Fabric of the Human Body*, which contained over 600 anatomical drawings and completely changed the way medics viewed the body.

This period of new, modern thinking inspired by Lucretius' poem had been growing in strength in central Europe for 200 years by the time it arrived in Britain in the 1500s. But coupled with the emergence of the new, early middle classes – the yeomen – and the increase in disposable income facilitated by the Black Death, it quickly took off. Renaissance achievements in England included the theatrical works of William Shakespeare and the polyphonic compositions of John Dunstable. But the impact of the Renaissance on medicine cannot be underestimated.

Between 1536 and 1541, Henry VIII dissolved 625 monasteries in England. Inspired by the grass roots reformation of religious practices in central Europe, and having had himself declared head of the English church in 1531 to facilitate a marriage annulment, Henry VIII's motives for religious reform were largely financial. He needed the assets to fund a war. But the knock-on effect of monastic closure resonated across English society. One of the major impacts was the loss of most of the religious hospitals, and a marked reduction in charity such as food and shelter for the poor. Over the next forty years, until the 1580s when a series of Poor Laws were passed, English philanthropy was reinvented as a private practice. Hospitals were taken over by wealthy benefactors, church colleges at the great universities were re-established, and alms houses were built by the rich to show their spiritual devotion. Faith and religious service had not been deposed, but monastic culture and the power of the papacy was all but destroyed. The new class of yeomen, created out of the chaos of the Black Death, took over as the givers of charity, and they also demanded professionalised medical care.

As English thought moved away from the church and toward the humanities, the landscape of medicine and welfare changed remarkably, setting the scene for public health reforms and new scientific discoveries that would themselves lay the foundation of the future British welfare state.

Chapter VI

Written in the Stars – Influenza from 1590 to 1918, and the Foundations of Modern Public Healthcare

'Looking up at his disciples, Jesus said: 'Blessed are you who are poor, for yours is the Kingdom of God. Blessed are you who hunger now, for you will be filled. Blessed are you who weep now, for you will laugh.'

Luke 6:20-21

How often do you look up at the stars? Do you love a dark night with a detailed Milky Way; a telescope focused on the bright light of Jupiter or Venus? Humans today are fascinated by the stars because we know what they are – distant, burning balls of gas and the planets that reflect the light of their nearest star. We know they flicker because of the effect the earth's atmosphere has on their light as it travels toward our greedy eyes. We know the night sky is a window to a universe so blindingly complex it continues to take the breath away of even the most learned scholar. The beauty of stars draws our eye, and the science keeps our brain engaged.

But in ancient times, humans turned to the stars for entirely different reasons. Early man saw the night sky as evidence of Gods, and tracked the phases of the moon as a way to keep time. The ancient Greeks began to map the sky and its seasonal changes. Man began to find meaning in the night sky, and even though that meaning was largely a human construct rather than anything tangible or scientific, it shaped society.

In the Middle Ages in Europe it was believed that celestial bodies influenced the health of people. The Latin word 'influentia' – meaning influence, or to flow into – was periodically used to describe outbreaks of illness which people believed were influenced by the stars. In 1357, the Italian version of the word, 'influenza', was used for the first time to describe a sickness that spread across Italy. After this, the word 'influenza' slowly became more common when describing illness. Because respiratory infections were more common at certain times of the year, it was felt the alignment of the night sky during that season played a key role. However, the world 'influenza' was not the name of the disease itself, but rather a concept relating to why the disease was occurring. People still saw these respiratory infections as being distinctly different from each other.

> On this day [13 July 1510] … in Modena there appeared an illness that lasts three days with a great fever, and headache and then they rise … but there remains a terrible cough that lasts maybe eight days, and then little by little they recover and do not perish.[1]

These are the words of Tommasino de' Bianchi, the author of one of only six first-hand accounts of a pandemic that swept Europe in 1510 that we now recognise as flu. In a paper on the 1510 pandemic published in *The Lancet* in 2010, authors Morens, North and Taubenberger state that flu as we understand it today had been circulating since the ninth century AD. Epidemics such as Italian Fever in AD 876, and the disease known as 'Sweate' between 1485 and 1551 were almost definitely influenza. Yet at the time the diseases were considered in singular terms, distinct from their historical cousins.

In 1557, a pandemic disease referred to as 'influenza' spread from Asia, to Africa, to Europe, the Ottoman Empire and even the Americas. It lasted for two years and not only killed a high number of people, but was directly linked to miscarriages. In 1580, an epidemic disease that spread through Europe was almost certainly related to modern influenza. Because of the way symptoms were recorded and gaps in the data, it can be hard to pin point the clinical details to know for sure the cause. But as time moved on the word influenza became intrinsically linked with the symptoms we recognise today as flu, and by the time of the epidemic in 1743 that caused the winter death toll in London to triple, the name influenza and its shortened version, 'flue' was in common parlance among the English. It was now considered one, reoccurring condition.

Flu began to hit more frequently, especially in the newly industrial cities of Western Europe in the eighteenth century. As medical thought moved away from faith and magic and became more focused on the natural word, the cause and origins of flu occupied some of the great minds of the time. In 1878, fowl plague – a type of flu in birds – was identified although not connected with the human disease. Shortly afterward the concept of a virus, a 'poison' smaller than a bacteria, was developed – although again, not connected with flu. As the calendar rolled over to the start of the twentieth century, much of the focus of healthcare was around tuberculosis and pneumonia, but nothing could prepare the world for what was about to happen, and how it would change the landscape of medical research for good.

In April 1916, 19-year-old Harry Underdown was helping his dad sow the fields of the family farm, Hodge End, in Kent, when a letter arrived. He'd signed up to the war effort the previous year, and now he was being called to duty. He reported to Surrey for training, no doubt excited and afraid like many young men before and after him. But unlike many of those men, Underdown's training was marred by sickness. He watched as group after group of new recruits completed their training and were sent off to fight in the trenches in Europe, at the height of the Great War. Underdown spent most of his time in Surrey in the hospital wing with repeated tonsillitis and other 'flu-like' infections.

It was February 1917 when he arrived at the sprawling military muster point at Étaples, on the coast of Northern France. Around 100,000 men were squashed into this camp, many of them having been sent there from the trenches with sickness and injury. A bronchial pneumonia had swept through the Front and many men were seriously ill. Harry Underdown was at the camp just a few days, waiting for his posting, when he began to notice a sore throat and a crackle in his chest. Less than two weeks later, Underwood was dead, a casualty of this mysterious pneumonia that had left military doctors baffled. The virulent disease appeared to cause a build-up of what many described at pus in the lungs of patients, preventing them from breathing. Underwood barely got to fire a shot on behalf of his country, and another 156 men died in similar circumstances by the end of the winter in Étaples. The cause of this disease was never explained.

Later in 1917, thousands of miles north-east of France, Dr Wu Lien-Teh was being called by Chinese authorities to visit the province of Shansi in Northern China. A British-trained doctor who had married the medical principles of the East and West in his practice, Lien-Teh had gained much respect after identifying and stopping a terrifying bout of plague in Harbin in 1910. His then unorthodox methods, such as conducting post-mortems and recommending cremations of the dead, had gone against Chinese cultural beliefs, but had also averted disaster and saved countless lives.

In Shansi, he saw all the tell-tale signs of plague – except that not everyone was dying. Few people who catch plague live to tell the tale, but in Shansi, just as many recovered as those who succumbed to this 'winter sickness'. Struggling to identify the disease which had already spread across 300 miles in just six weeks, Lien-Teh tried to enact the same protocol as had saved many in Harbin: quarantine. But local authorities weren't supportive of the move and he was chased out of the region when he attempted to perform a post-mortem on a victim without the family's consent.

Back in Beijing, the new government of the Republic of China weren't happy with the results of Lien-Teh's visit to Shansi. They were profiting from the war by sending Chinese workers to the front line to support Allied efforts with hard labour. Since 1916, 94,000 Chinese men had been sent to the muster point at Étaples to work at digging trenches and heavy lifting, as part of the Chinese Labour Corps. Evidence of sickness in these men had been played down by authorities to keep the war effort running smoothly, and the last thing the Chinese government wanted now was a fuss. Lien-Teh had lost their respect and was side-lined. No quarantine measures were put in place, and the 'winter sickness' was hushed up until it began to disperse in the spring of 1918.

Almost exactly one year after Harry Underdown died, on the second Monday of March 1918, Private Albert Gitchell became unwell at Fort Riley, Kansas. Like Underdown, Gitchell was also training to be sent to the Front with American troops, when he found himself struck by a fever. He reported to the medical team at Fort Riley, and promptly passed out. If he had stayed conscious, he would have seen man after man admitted in the days after him with similar aggressive symptoms. Historians would later note that in the days after Gitchell's admission to hospital, men in military camps across America were taken ill with similar symptoms – as well as some who had already been shipped off to Europe.

About 300 miles south of Fort Riley, Dr Loring Milner, a local physician in Haskell Country, Kansas, was being run ragged in his horse-drawn buggy. He was seeing domestic patients struck down with similar symptoms to the ones that had struck Gitchell. Although it was being nicknamed by the farming community 'knock me down fever', due to the speed and veracity with which the illness started, Dr Milner recognised it as influenza, and was prescribing fluids and bedrest to all the patients he saw. But not all his patients were responding in the usual way. While some recovered as expected after several days, others died a horrible, painful and protracted death, unable to breathe due to the mucus build up in their lungs. And while some of the dead were vulnerable elderly patients, some were also young women, and strapping young men in the prime of their life. This was not the usual pattern for flu, and it troubled the doctor greatly.

The virus that gripped the world in a lethal pandemic between 1918 and 1920 was known at the time as Spanish flu, although the name was an accident of circumstance. The Spanish were not involved in the First World War, and so they had no media blackout. When people began dropping like flies with a mystery influenza in Madrid – including King Alfonso XIII – foreign papers quickly picked up on the news reports to fill their column inches. Wartime media suppression meant domestic incidences of the disease could not be reported at home, but word of this new 'Spanish influenza' spread.

Of course, the disease did not originate in Spain. The first reports of it there weren't until late May 1918, a long time after the first signs of it had been noted elsewhere. But over 100 years later, despite theories of origin from France, China and the USA, we still don't really know where in the world it emerged from. We didn't even know for sure it was a virus until 1931, when the electron microscope made it possible to see viruses for the first time.

At the time of the pandemic, the cause was thought to be Pfeiffer's bacillus, a bacterial infection. Richard Pfeiffer was a protégé of Robert Koch, and had identified this bacteria in the throat of flu patients during the influenza epidemic of 1889–92. There was even a vaccine for it – although of course it had limited success, as it really only helped reduce the impact of secondary infections.

Between 1932 and 1933, British scientists Wilson Smith, Sir Christopher Andrewes and Sir Patrick Laidlaw isolated influenza virus 'A' from the nasal mucus of infected patients. In the 1940s, influenza type 'B' was discovered, as were small variations in the original 'A' type virus.

This was the first indication of the flu virus's ability to mutate, creating more and less dangerous strains. We now know there are four types of influenza virus, A, B, C and D, with various subtypes in each. It's the A and B strains that affect humans, and it is only the A strains that cause pandemics. Spanish flu is now recognised as the H1N1 subtype of influenza A, with the letters and numbers corresponding to the number of hemagglutinin and neuraminidase proteins. Originally an avian flu that infected humans, a version of it was acquired by pigs and then re-entered the human population in 2009, and we called it 'swine flu'.

But all this knowledge couldn't answer a simple question – why had Spanish flu killed 100 million people, or 5 per cent of the world's population at the time? There were lots of hypothesis: information suppression relating to the war meant people weren't prepared; populations like Western Samoa had no acquired immunity causing a greater death toll; the unprecedented movement and mixing of people. This all explained the spread, but didn't really explain the virility – or the fact that it was healthy young people who suffered most, unlike with other flu outbreaks. It wasn't until a retired physician visited the arctic in the late 1990s that the pieces of the puzzle were finally put together.

San Francisco based Johan Hultin had visited the isolated northern enclave called Brevig Mission, Alaska, in the 1950s. During the pandemic, 90 per cent of the population of Brevig Mission had been killed by the Spanish flu. After reading about a failed attempt by a team from the University of Windsor, Canada, to extract a sample of the virus from frozen bodies in Norway, Hutlin contacted well-known US virologist Jeffery Taubenberger with a plan. Hutlin then visited Brevig Mission, obtained permission from the Mayor to open a mass grave from 1918 with the help of local muscle, extracted a sample of genetic material from the bodies buried in the permafrost using a set of his wife's sterilised pruning shears, and sent it in a special serum to Taubenberger via courier post.

This low-profile, low-cost expedition garnered little attention at the time, but when Taubenberger got his hands on the serum, and explained to US authorities he intended to rebuild the genetic code, things started to heat up. Eventually, he was given permission by the National Science Advisory Board for Biosafety in the USA, provided he used a secure facility with highly trained staff and never published the genetic code, lest the virus be used in warfare. When Taubenberger managed to put the eight segments of genetic code back together he must have felt a bit green. Every single segment was lethal. One segment alone could have turned any pedestrian flu virus into a killer, but all eight together presented a highly toxic super virus that perhaps should have come with a greater death toll.

The virus Taubenberger was looking at had the ability to trigger cytokine storms in infected patients. This is a process where an overstimulated immune system starts to attack the body's own healthy cells instead of just the infected ones. It was this that was causing the lungs full of mucus in patients in the 1918 outbreak – the lining of the lungs was being dissolved by the body's own immune response. It also meant that the very healthy were actually more vulnerable. This strain could also block interferons, a signal protein that works as an early warning system. Infected cells send out interferons so other cells can bolster their immune response in preparation for the virus's attack – but the H1N1 Spanish flu strain was able to prevent that early warning system from going off. Other factors included the virus's ability to replicate itself quickly, and how easily it was spread through coughs and sneezes.

The research Taubenberger and his team did over nine years changed the face of flu research and our understanding of how to protect ourselves and respond medically to such diseases. It has also changed the way we look for possible pandemics, with scientists seeking out new influenza A strains and mapping them at a molecular level to see what risk they pose.

Back in 1918 though, our forefathers didn't have any of this information. All they knew was that people were dropping like flies with this mysterious disease. The impact of the flu pandemic on public health strategy around the globe, both short term and long term, cannot be understated.

In Washington DC, 6-year-old William Sardo gasped at the coffins lining the hall and living room of his home. His dad was an undertaker, the funeral home attached to the back of their house. By October 1918, they had become so overwhelmed by the number of people dying they had to bring the coffins inside. A combination of the volume of people who were succumbing to the flu, coupled with a lack of grave diggers meant that laying the dead to rest was slow. The next challenge happened when there was a lack of caskets. With the hospitals and morgues jam-packed, people were dying at home, bodies laid out on the dining room tables and desperate relatives begging the city for help.

District Health Officer William Fowler solved the coffin problem by commandeering a shipment meant for Pittsburgh. He solved the grave digger problem by getting prisoners involved. And ultimately, he reduced the spread of the disease by closing schools and banning public gatherings, and handing out free gauze masks to residents. But nearby New York took a totally different approach, relying on the concept of 'civic duty' to manage the epidemic. Although the port was a hot spot for infection, the city was under pressure from the military not to close or quarantine it. This is just one of many examples of the war effort being prioritised over public health. Equally, in the city itself, efforts to restrict public movement and stem the spread of the disease were not made until two months after the first cases. Even then, there were no shop closures or bans on public gatherings. Instead, staggered opening times for businesses was introduced, and influenza was made a reportable disease – it was the public's responsibility to not get on a crowded subway, and let the authorities know if they were sick. Schools and theatres remained open, and President Woodrow Wilson even led a parade through the streets in the same week as 2,000 city residents died from flu. Their major public health concession was the opening of 150 medical centres for the infected to receive treatment.

In Philadelphia, Spanish flu was introduced in September via a military ship en route from Boston – a city heavily affected by the epidemic. Insisting the illness was 'La Grippe', a common, generic flu, city authorities did absolutely nothing to try and quarantine the port or prevent the spread of disease into the city.

On 28 September, despite a worrying increase in the infection rate and flu now being a reportable disease, a Liberty Loan drive to raise money for the military was allowed to go ahead. Record numbers of people took to the streets, 200,000 people lining up to watch a parade that stretched for two miles. Forty-eight hours later, 635 new cases of Spanish flu were reported in a single day. By the end of the week there were more than 200,000 cases in the city, with 300 deaths in just twenty-four hours.

Although schools were closed and public gatherings banned, it was too little too late. Morgues were packed tight and funerals postponed on safety grounds. Racial segregation meant that in the African-American districts of the city where people could not access medical care, 2,000 nuns had set up emergency field hospitals. At one centre a trench was dug outside for the bodies because there was nowhere else for them to go. Just ten days after the Liberty Loan drive, the city was on its knees, essential services collapsed. The telephones were barely functioning because 850 employees had not shown up for work, and 500 police officers were off sick. Military doctors and embalmers were drafted in for support and families were digging their own loved-ones' graves.

These tragic stories from the USA were repeated in cities across the world. In Auckland, the *New Zealand Herald* wrongly reported the war was over on 8 November 1918. A crowd took to the streets despite warnings to stay at home to stop the spread of the killer flu virus, which had arrived a month before. People got out of their sick bed to celebrate, coughing and spluttering among the singing crowd on Queen Street in the city centre. The celebrations were eventually shut down by police acting on a public health decree, but sadly much of the damage had already been done. A few days later when the real armistice was announced, the only activity on the streets were funeral processions, a city centre park used as a makeshift morgue.

In Western Samoa, 20 per cent of the local population died from Spanish flu that came from a military ship in the port. With no level of acquired immunity against flu viruses, which are a European-centric disease, Samoans practically fell where they stood. In India, the Ganges river was bloated with bodies left there by families who could not afford a funeral pyre. The poet Nirala recalled this devastating sight later in life. He had been returning home after completing his studies in Calcutta, the smell of death following him as he made his way to his in-laws house where he discovered his young wife had just died. In northern Canada, entire Inupiat villages were found empty of life, but corpses were locked together in churches and school rooms. This is a decision victims must have made while they were still conscious, understanding their fate and not wanting their bodies to be eaten by the dogs.

In the UK, by the week of the 19 May 1918 the pandemic was in full swing. There were 511 recorded deaths that week compared to seventy-nine the week before – a jump of 546 per cent. By the end of June, the deaths of young people outweighed the deaths of the over 55 age bracket[2] and it was clear that what was happening was a formidable event, not just a virulent seasonal virus doing the rounds. We all know the accepted plague origin story of the playground song 'ring-a-ring o'roses', but now the school children were singing a different rhyme:

> I had a little bird,
> Its name was Enza,
> I opened-up the window,
> And in – flew – enza.

The impact on the population, already malnourished and depressed from four long years of the loss and hardship of war, was significant. In July 1918, *The Times* reported that some coalmines in Newcastle had 70 per cent of their workforce off sick. At the start of August, the coalfields in Wigan were operating with just two-thirds of the required workforce. Bus and train services had to be reduced and postponed due to staff sickness, Post Offices and bakeries were operating reduced hours and – similar to in the US – undertakers were turning down work because they were literally stacked with bodies.

By the time the second wave hit in the autumn of 1918, the medical profession was under a lot of pressure. If you couldn't afford to pay privately, then healthcare at this time was provided largely according to the English Poor Laws, which dated back to the Middle Ages. The most significant – and controversial – update, the Poor Law Amendment Act, had been passed in parliament almost 100 years before Spanish flu arrived, in 1834. Taking the view that people were the cause of their own poverty, rather than the socio-economic conditions present at the time, it set out to simply make it undesirable to be poor. Workhouses became the only source of help and were made deliberately inhospitable to discourage their use. Outdoor relief, the process of giving people financial aid, food and clothing during periods of unemployment, was also outlawed – which was problematic for seasonal workers – and mothers of illegitimate children were prevented from claiming financial assistance from the father to discourage lust.

There was a lot of social resistance to these new Poor Laws, and over the eighty-four years between it passing and the outbreak of Spanish flu, there were many more smaller changes made, focused on righting some of the wrongs of the initial act. One thing that didn't fully change until 1918, however, was Poor Relief Disenfranchisement. If you claimed help from the workhouse, including medical help in some cases, you could lose your right to vote.

These laws meant that historically, those who needed help were often reluctant to claim it. Even when changes were made, such as the Medical

Relief Disqualification Removal Act of 1845, which meant those who claimed poor-rate healthcare without entering the workhouse system fully could retain most of their democratic rights, they were often poorly communicated, not well understood, or simply not effectively applied by the authorities. A good example is that free school meals and access to medical care for children were legally introduced by the new Liberal government from 1907 to try and improve general health, but it was not compulsory for local authorities to comply, and so these changes were largely ignored.

By the early twentieth century, people had begun turning to other initiatives for support when on hard times, including when sick. Friendly Societies were popular among those who could afford membership, with some of the benefits including access to a doctor and funeral costs covered by the society. Trade Unions also often supplied access to healthcare for members – but it was common for the women and children of a worker to be excluded. Although workhouse-based infirmaries were still the only port of call for the truly destitute, the 1911 National Insurance Act meant that those who were employed (mostly men) could at least claim sick pay and see a doctor for free.

When the Spanish flu hit the UK, access to healthcare was the best it had ever been, but by today's standards it was irregular and inequitable. In addition, many medical doctors and nurses had been seconded to military hospitals or sent overseas. The hospitals were not staffed or equipped for a mass outbreak. Women who weren't working were usually not eligible for any free health provision, and many councils just ignored children entirely. It should perhaps come as no surprise then that the mortality rate for women was high. One piece of research showed that the death rate in women aged 25–30 was 600 times higher in 1918 than in the previous four years. Pregnant women were twice as likely to develop pneumonic complications.

Some younger patients who arrived in hospital, suffering from the effects of the not yet understood cytokine storm, could be dead within a day. They then became the problem of the morgue, who were having their own resourcing crisis. Older and younger patients however were not as vulnerable to an overactive immune system response. They might take weeks to either recover, or die. Although there is a lack of official statistics on the issue, the sharp rise in the number of orphans has been anecdotally noted. Three new, national, philanthropic organisations dedicated to finding orphaned children a new home were established in 1918, presumably to deal with this increase.

When it came to survival rates, statistics show that people who lived in towns in the UK were up to 40 per cent more likely to die from the Spanish flu[3] than people living rurally. This could have been because there was better access to medical care in the country, such as a dedicated local doctor. It could also have been related to better air quality. Dr Leonard Hill at London Hospital's Medical School insisted patients have access to fresh air, cool and dry. He said if necessary, they should sleep outside and some makeshift tent hospitals offered better recovery rates in their stats than the traditional bricks and mortar, sealed window, heating-blasting model of British infirmary. During the official forty-six weeks of the pandemic in the UK, the Registrar General recorded over 170,000 deaths, but it is widely considered the real total is closer to 220,000.

The legacy of Spanish flu was further changes to social support that would lead to the welfare state after the Second World War thirty years later. Although it is heart-warming to think of Britain as this altruistic, burgeoning socialist state, a major driving force for these measures was post-war productivity and the need for financial recovery. Researchers have estimated the UK's GDP fell by 5 to 6 per cent as a result of the pandemic. In January 1919, Prudential Insurance Company noted between 2 November and 31 December 1918, £650,000 was paid out to cover industrial losses from flu. In the same period, just £279,000 was paid out to cover losses caused by the war. It is a vignette that illustrates the dire need for measures to prevent disease, improve public health and keep people at work.

Health and housing were suddenly top of the agenda. Between 1918 and 1921, out of work payments were made available to the unemployed, and in 1919 the Addison Act financed the building of good quality housing for council tenants. Also, passed in 1919 was the Ministry of Health Act, which established a health minister and government office for national health for the first time. Its role was to 'take all such steps as may be desirable to secure the preparation, effective carrying out and coordination of measures conducive to the health of the people.'[4] As well as public health service provision, the new Ministry of Health was in charge of housing, pensions, the national insurance scheme and environmental health – a clear indicator of the new holistic, strategic thinking of government when it came to the health of citizens. The Medical Research Council (MRC) was also established in that year, usurping a smaller commission set up in 1901 to research tuberculosis specifically. The new MRC began researching more broadly, making the flu virus a priority.

In 1925, an act to support widows, orphans and pensioners was passed, with the Unemployment Assistance Board established in 1934. The 1929 Local Government Act superseded most of the Poor Laws. These measures were even more necessary as the hedonism of the 1920s gave way to depression, culminating in the miners' strike of 1926. Some unions went bankrupt, and some Friendly Societies couldn't function financially, which meant that lower paid workers and the unemployed relied on public hospitals. But there was still a stigma attached to them, especially as many continued to be part of workhouse estates, and legislators began to try and reduce it by changing the language used to describe state assistance.

The ongoing health impacts of Spanish flu meant it was essential people started to live and work in healthier environments. Many people who recovered from the virus were left with lifelong heart and lung problems, and some people had central nervous system issues as well. Children born during or just after Spanish flu were, statistically speaking, physically shorter, and more likely to suffer from childhood diseases than their counterparts born just a few years before. The state had begun to realise before the war that it needed to look after people better for everybody's sake. Spanish flu made further intervention an economic necessity – although the NHS as we know it today didn't arrive until 1948.

The new Liberal government of the early twentieth century had set out changes in the years before the war that would effectively become the infrastructure of today's social services, but it took the joint impact of a pandemic during a war to really move society toward the welfare state.

Chapter VII

Free Healthcare at the Point of Use
The Birth of the UK NHS

'No society can legitimately call itself civilised if a sick person is denied medical aid because of lack of means.'

Aneurin 'Nye' Bevan, *In Place of Fear*, 1952

My mum has a favourite story from her childhood. The type that makes her eyes sparkle with nostalgia and joy. My mum grew up in a large, boisterous family, living in a small, east London flat. It wasn't unusual for an injury to occur – as often as daily on occasion. And when it did, or if one of the kids had a sore throat or high temperature, my nan would put them in a pushchair (even if they were quite old) and run them down the street to the GP with all the other kids trying to keep up, a cloud of dust and limbs chasing our hero. In my head, whenever my mum told this story to me as a child, I imagined my aunty or uncle semi-conscious in the buggy, and my nan would be wearing a flashing blue light on her head, just like an ambulance.

This story conjures up many things. It is the image of the caring, frazzled mother. It is a feminist treatise in miniature – after all, my grandad was a seasonal worker with chunks of downtime, but he never features in these childcare vignettes. It of course demonstrates how important the NHS was to that post-war generation. My mum and her siblings were born between 1944 and 1958, and so they enjoyed what many would call the glory days of this new 'free' healthcare service and never knew any different.

It also contains a subtext that I definitely missed as a child. In that vision in my head there is a look of desperation on my nan's face as she rushes her precious darling to medical aid. But I was wrong, I think. Now, I realise that this working-class woman, born in 1924, who grew up and got married and lived through a world war with no guarantee of medical help should she need it would not have been feeling desperate, but grateful. The look on her face is relief. Finally, she was able to access the help she needed from a doctor without worrying about the up-front cost or availability of care. Most importantly, she knew her children would always have the medical help they needed, as and when they needed it – help her own family had no doubt been denied by their finances in my nan's youth.

Aneurin Bevan, known as Nye, was the post-war Labour MP responsible for ushering in the NHS. He was the generation above my nan. Born in 1897, he muddled through school, with much of his learning happening on his own terms in the local library.[1] Along with two thirds of the men in his village of Tredegar in Monmouthshire, South Wales, he began working in a local colliery aged 14. His life was destined to be average and unremarkable. Like his father before him he had a career labouring in the coal mines practically written on his birth certificate.

But despite a stammer and a visual impairment that prevented him from serving in the Great War, Bevan was not one to toe the line. Frequently dismissed from jobs for complaining about poor working conditions or money saving decisions that could put the men in the pits at risk, he found himself labelled as a trouble maker, and as a result was unemployed for several years in the 1920s. It was during this time that his father, a lifelong miner, died in Bevan's arms from pneumoconiosis – an industrial disease caused by inhaling coal dust.

In a 2008 documentary about Nye Bevan, Former BBC Director General Greg Dyke suggests the death of Bevan's father was a pivotal moment in the young politician-to-be's life, a moment in which he dreamed up a system of free at the point of use health care available to everyone in the UK. It seems from other accounts of his life that Bevan himself was not prone to this sort of self-reflection, but it is likely that his father's death had a huge impact on both his interest in politics, and the direction of his political beliefs. In 1926, he found work as a union official, and during the General Strike that year he emerged as a leader. In 1928, he began his journey to parliament by winning a seat on the Monmouthshire County Council.

Bevan says himself, in the opening chapter of his 1952 book *In Place of Fear*:

I started my political life with no clearly formed personal ambition ... I leave that nonsense to the writers of romantic biographies. A young miner in a South Wales Colliery, my concern was with the one practical question, where does power lie in this particular State of Great Britain, and how can it be attained by the worker?

He saw his role, his mission in life, to level the playing field between the rich and the poor. To allow democracy to flourish through the simple act of giving every citizen access to the things they needed. Good homes, safe jobs, and free healthcare were high on his list, and while it might be a stretch to picture him dreaming of that equity as his father lay dying before him, there is no doubt that his roots in South Wales had a major influence on the direction he took, especially with healthcare.

In 1890, the 'Tredegar Workmen's Medical Aid and Sick Relief Fund' was formed, a collaboration between a number of existing groups and societies that supported the local population. They opened a cottage hospital in 1904, with local working men agreeing to contribute a small amount of their salary each week to make the provision possible. By 1911 the society was well known and well regarded nationally, an example of one of the most comprehensive worker support societies of its kind in the UK. Later known just as the Tredegar Workmen's Medical Aid Society, by the 1920s it had around 20,000 members, and offered the services of five doctors, one surgeon, two pharmacists, a physiotherapist, a dentist and a district nurse. It has long been credited as the model on which the NHS was based, with Bevan saying in a 1947 speech about the nationalisation of a health service; 'All I am doing is extending to the entire population of Britain the benefits we had in Tredegar for a generation or more. We are going to Tredegar-ise you.'

In a 2018 article in *The Conversation*, Steve Thompson, a senior lecturer in History at Aberystwyth University, says that the notion the NHS was based on the Tredegar outfit is an over simplification of what really unfolded. While the Tredegar-worker-owned-and-controlled health insurance system certainly holds a very close resemblance to the NHS launched in 1948, he says it is impossible to ignore the other important steps toward socialist healthcare that we've seen in previous chapters. Thompson notes that the Liberal reforms of the early twentieth century, including the worker health insurance system introduced in 1911, the voluntary hospital system, and the medical arm of the older Poor Law, all set up the foundations of the NHS and contributed to the final model – even if that contribution was to right a previous wrong. The inequity caused by the exclusion of wives and children from the health insurance system, for example, was resolved with the nationalisation of health care in the UK.

The way the Tredegar Society worked can definitely be seen as a blueprint for the way the NHS worked in its early days, with even the sundries of medical aid like wigs and prosthetic limbs readily covered. The aim of the NHS was to holistically improve the quality of life for British people. It wasn't an empty promise or political point scorer, it actually delivered. But as we have seen, the road to this point had been long, with many leaps of faith and changes of direction.

The creation of the NHS can and should be viewed as revolutionary, but it certainly wasn't sudden. Centuries of public health laws and social welfare reforms contributed to that moment in 1948 when healthcare became accessible to all. But that doesn't mean the result of the change wasn't incredible for many people. For some British people, like the residents of Tredegar, little may have changed except that they were paying into a national system rather than a local one. But for those previously excluded from such a system, either geographically, or because they didn't work, or because their union hadn't set one up or at least one not as comprehensive as in other areas, the change to their life would have been immediate and profound. But arguably, although the seeds of the welfare state had been germinating for some time by 1948, the change would not have been so easily accepted by all tiers of society and political leanings, had it not been for the Second World War.

Before the war, the idea of eugenics had been gaining ground. In 1883 Sir Francis Galton, a cousin of Charles Darwin, proposed the idea that the human race could strategically direct its evolution in a positive direction through selective breeding. The word eugenics was coined by Galton and is derived from the Greek words 'eu', meaning 'well' or 'good', and 'genes', meaning 'born'.

Galton was inspired both by Darwin's *On the Origin of Species* and by the writings of embryologist August Weismann, who studied hereditary traits. But both Darwin and Weismann believe that while natural selection was real, it was not something that was possible – or even desirable – to control. Galton disagreed. He felt that humans should be breeding in order to increase the chances of perpetuating 'desirable traits' – but what constitutes a desirable trait was then and still is, rightfully, in dispute. While early supporters of eugenics focused their thoughts around desirability on classist ideas of intelligence, it soon began to descend into conversations around racial pseudoscience and also, discriminating against those with disability.

It is not hard to see why eugenics is discriminatory, but the real danger of course is in who controls that discrimination, and for what purpose. Laws preventing those who were considered 'mentally deficient' from having children had been in place for some time in England, not overtly but through the practice of separating men and women living in institutions. Arguably, the poor in the workhouses were also subjected to a type of eugenics, as they were also separated into sex-based dorms. But these soft, blurry prejudices hiding behind a philanthropic facade gave way to bold justification of exclusion through breeding in the years leading up to the war.

Nowhere is this perhaps more obvious than in Australia's 'Stolen Generations'. Between 1905 and 1967 an overt Aboriginal child removal policy existed, with as many as 70 per cent of children being removed from some Aboriginal communities. Initially focused on the removal of 'mixed-descent' children with white fathers, in some parts of Australia children of aboriginal descent, especially girls, could also be removed from their community and raised either in specialist homes or adopted by white families. White Australians often had legal jurisdiction over the lives of these children until they were 21, making decisions such as where they were allowed to live and work and who they could marry.

Underpinning this policy was an assumption that the Aboriginal people were, or would, become extinct. The Native Affairs Minister, a British man named A.O. Neville, did little to hide his ambition to breed Aboriginals out of existence. Neville believed in a natural racial hierarchy, and that Europeans were superior to the first nation peoples of Australia. He, and others in government, saw the absorption of the Aboriginal people in to the 'white race' as a way of unifying Australia.

Back in Britain, the pre-war eugenics movement was less about race and more about disability. Advocates wanted to breed a stronger society by offering incentives for young healthy couples to have a family, and to legislate against the physically and mentally 'feeble' from procreating. It will probably surprise most people on the left wing of politics now, to discover the huge level of support for eugenics among socialists. Beatrice and Sidney Webb, the founders of the Fabian society, were huge fans of the idea, as was Labour Party member and economist Harold Laski. Socialist liberal Bertrand Russell proposed that people be issued colour-coded tickets dictating who was allowed to breed with whom, with fines in place for people who flouted the rules. Those on the far right also supported these ideas as a means of mass control. Opposition to eugenics generally came from the individualistic libertarians.

In an article for the *New Statesman*, Victoria Brignell notes that in 1908, Sir James Crichton-Brown gave evidence to the Royal Commission on the Care and Control of the Feeble-Minded, which described those with learning disabilities and mental illness as 'our social rubbish' and recommended they be forcibly sterilised. Winston Churchill agreed with him. He actually attended the first International Eugenics Conference which was held in London in 1912. Labour MP Will Crooks is often fondly remembered for his campaigning work against poverty and inequality. His father had lost an arm in an industrial accident, and Crooks was educated at a Poor Law school with some of his siblings entering the workhouse. Even so, he held divisive views about disability, describing so-called 'mentally defective' children as 'like human vermin ... polluting and corrupting everything they touch' in a speech in parliament in 1912. In the same speech he advocated for state control over people who could not look after themselves. While he emphasised their humanity, stating that their lives can and should be improved, he finished with the chilling phrase, 'above everything else, you would stop the supply of these children'[2] – a clear nod toward eugenics and an illustration of the complex entanglement of beliefs held by those who wanted to improve society for all, but felt this could best be done by eliminating some of those who were seen to be pulling everyone else down.

Perhaps the most surprising supporter of eugenics retrospectively was William Beveridge, the author of the Beveridge Report (the official title is Social Insurance and the Allied Services) which first proposed the idea of a public health service that would care for people 'from cradle to the grave'. But Beveridge was no socialist. He was a Liberal and he believed that by eradicating what he called the Five Giant Evils –

want, disease, ignorance, squalor and idleness, society would be more productive economically speaking. In that context, his eugenics leanings make perfect sense. The report recommendations include setting up a National Health Service to help counter the evils of disease and want, in conjunction with other recommendations relating to the welfare state. Although ultimately about increasing GDP rather than improving the individual's lot in life, in the hands of the Labour party, and in the context of the late war and early post-war period, the treatment of the report and the implementation of its recommendations was definitely handled more with social good in mind, as well as social recovery.

The Beveridge Report was published in November 1942, in the glaring heat of a cataclysmic global war and the mood of the public was definitely changing. Before the war, the idea of designing a society to be genetically strong, and to have that design controlled by the government, seemed like common sense. But the idea of human free will, independence and choice died a horrible death in the well of that sentiment – a death illustrated by the Nazi regime. People began to distance themselves from those ideas now seen as highly undesirable and associated with fascism.

The war also meant that a greater value was placed on individual liberty and freedom, and disability – particularly physical disability – became more common both in returning soldiers and among civilians who were victims of the Blitz. The loss of a limb, in particular, became an accepted part of everyday life and not something to be feared. In fact, those who had been disabled by war were greeted by most with respect and pride.

Although Churchill had not been keen on the Beveridge Report being made public in 1942 for financial reasons, as the leader of the wartime coalition government he can be credited with helping the passage of many welfare reforms. For example, maternity services in public hospitals were expanded, and the introduction of the National Milk Scheme in 1940 meant pregnant and nursing mothers could get free or heavily subsidised milk – at a time when dairy products were in short supply. From 1943, the idea of reconstruction in post-war Britain finally had a seat at the political table – Churchill had previously been very avoidant of talking about what happened after the war ended. But he appointed a Minister for Reconstruction and a committee was organised.

The Beveridge Report, which sold 70,000 copies in its first month, was exceptionally popular among the people of Britain. So popular in

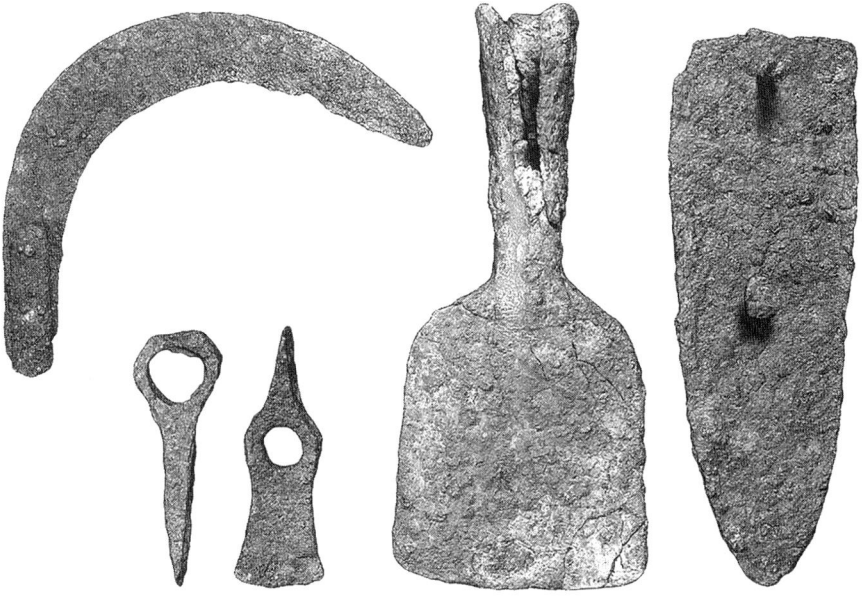

Ancient farming tools from the fertile crescent. (Wikimedia Commons)

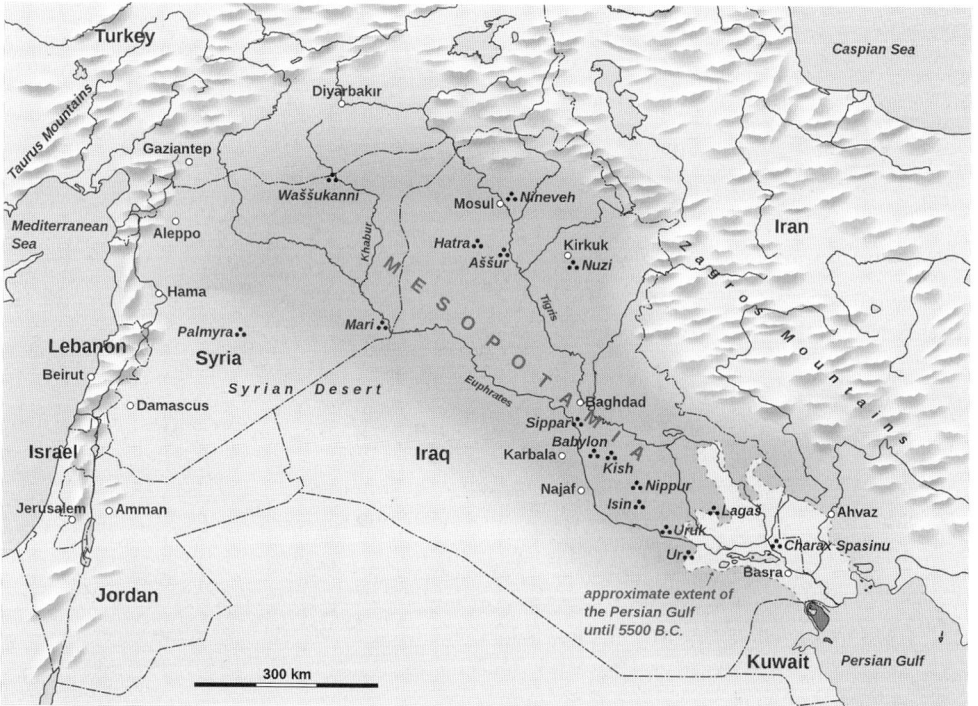

This map shows the location and extent of the Fertile Crescent, a region in the Middle East incorporating Ancient Egypt, the Levant and Mesopotamia. (Wikimedia Commons)

The angel of death striking a door during the plague of Rome. Engraving by J.G. Levasseur after J. Delaunay. (Wikimedia Commons)

Ancient Greek historian Thucydides – this is the plaster cast bust currently in exposition of Zurab Tsereteli's gallery in Moscow (part of Russian Academy of Arts), formerly from the collection of castings of Pushkin museum made in early 1900-1910s. Original bust is a Roman copy (c. 100 CE) of an early fourth century BCE Greek original, and is located in Holkham Hall in Norfolk, UK. (Wikimedia Commons)

Hippocrates of Kos; the 'father of medicine' – by unidentified engraver – 1881. (Wikimedia Commons)

A Greek vase from circa 470 BC depicting a physician treating a patient. Red-figure Attic aryballos. On display at the Louvre, Paris. (Wikimedia Commons)

A depiction of Emperor Justinian
Meister von San Vitale in Ravenna.
(Public domain image)

This 18th Dynasty Egyptian carving
is thought to show a polio victim.
(Wikimedia Commons)

St Bartholemew's main entrance, the Henry VIII Gate, built in the seventeenth century. All the medeaval buildings have now been replaced.

Plague panel from early seventeenth century Augsburg with a skull and crossbones with leaf crown. Panels of this kind were placed on the walls of houses to warn against the plague. A plague epidemic raged in Augsburg between 1607 and 1636. (Public domain image)

Galen of Pergamon, by Georg Paul Busch (engraver). (Wikimedia Commons)

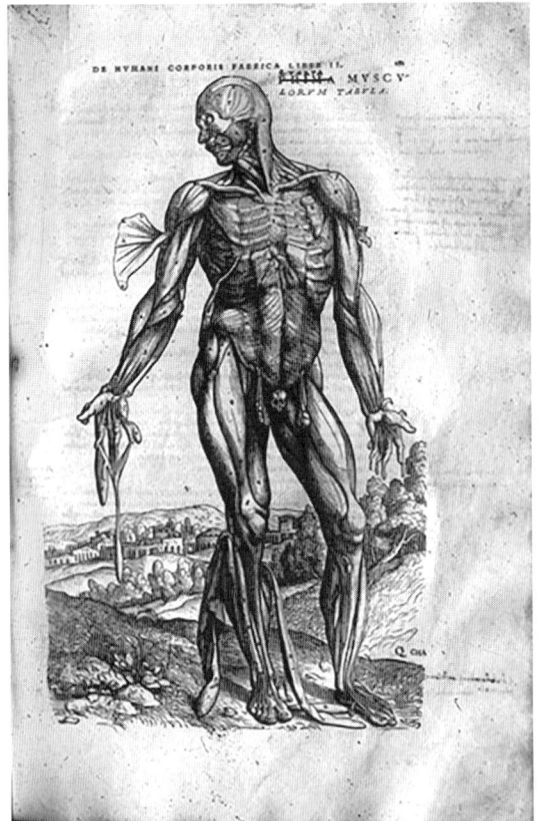

This is a picture taken from the online scans of Vesalius' book *De humanis fabricas corpus*, from the University of Oklahoma History of Science Collection records. It is an image of the muscular anatomy of a man. (Wikimedia Commons)

The Paris Catacombes house the remains of between 6 and 7 million people, five storeys underground. They were created in the seventeenth century after pressure was put on the cities burial grounds by the sheer number of bodies generated by bubonic plague.

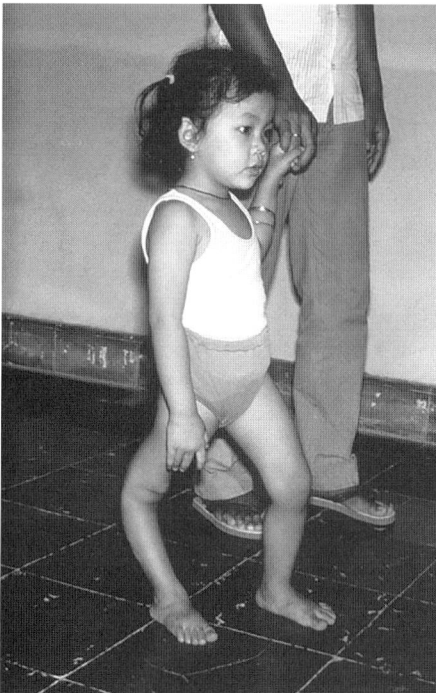

Polio sequelle. A child with a leg deformity due to polio, 1995. (Wikimedia Commons)

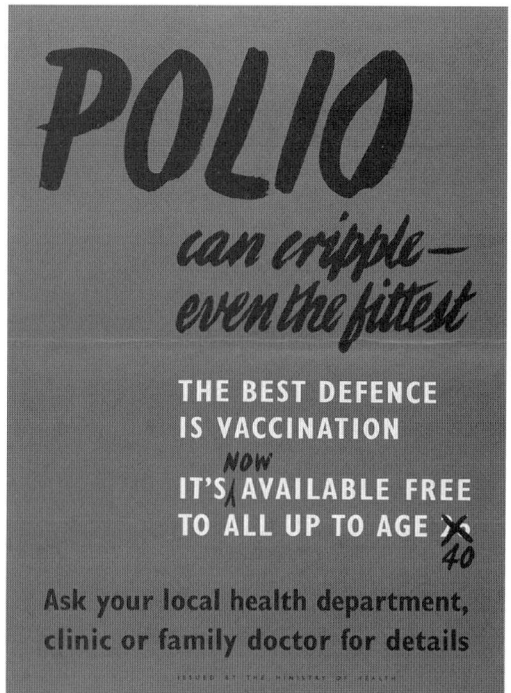

A British poster created as part of a government vaccination campaign in the 1950s. (Wellcome Collection)

Polio patient in an iron lung at the Scots Mission Hospital in Tiberias, Palestine in March 1940. When polio weakened muscles used in breathing, an iron lung assisted respiration. (Everett Collection, Shutterstock)

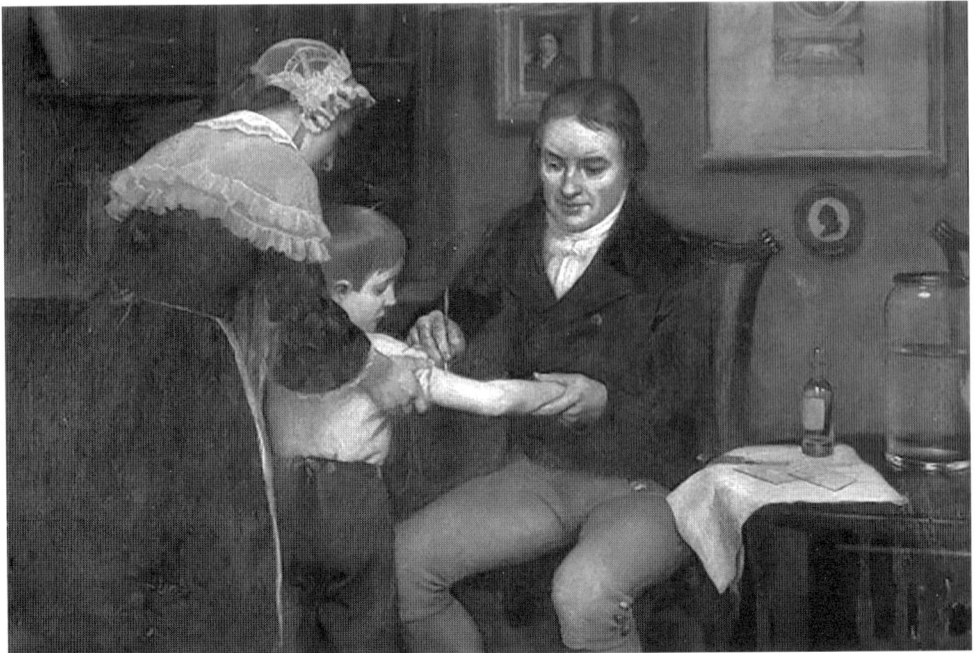

Dr Jenner performing his first vaccination on James Phipps, an 8-year-old boy; 14 May 1796. Ernest Board. (Wikimedia Commons)

The Cow-Pock — or — the Wonderful Effects of the New Inoculation! — Vide. the Publications of ye Anti-Vaccine Society.

The Cow-Pock—or—the Wonderful Effects of the New Inoculation!—vide. the Publications of ye Anti-Vaccine Society Print (color engraving) published 12 June, 1802 by H. Humphrey, St James's Street. In this cartoon, the British satirist James Gillray caricatured a scene at the Smallpox and Inoculation Hospital at St Pancras, showing cowpox vaccine being administered to frightened young women, and cows emerging from different parts of people's bodies. The cartoon was inspired by the controversy over inoculating against the dreaded disease, smallpox. Opponents of vaccination had depicted cases of vaccinees developing bovine features and this is picked up and exaggerated by Gillray. Although the central figure is often assumed to be Edward Jenner, circumstantial evidence suggests this may not be so. Although the director of the Smallpox Hospital, William Woodville, had originally supported Jenner, he and his colleague George Pearson were in dispute with Jenner by the time the caricature was published. It is unlikely they would have met Jenner and it has been suggested that the central figure represents Pearson. Gillray often included clues to identify individuals who were not easily recognisable, but the only clue here is the badge on the arm of the boy which identifies his connection with Woodville's hospital. The boy holds a container labelled 'VACCINE POCK hot from ye COW' and papers in the boy's pocket are labelled 'Benefits of the Vaccine'. The tub on the desk is labelled 'OPENING MIXTURE'. A bottle next to the tub is labelled 'VOMIT'. The painting on the wall depicts worshippers of the Golden Calf.

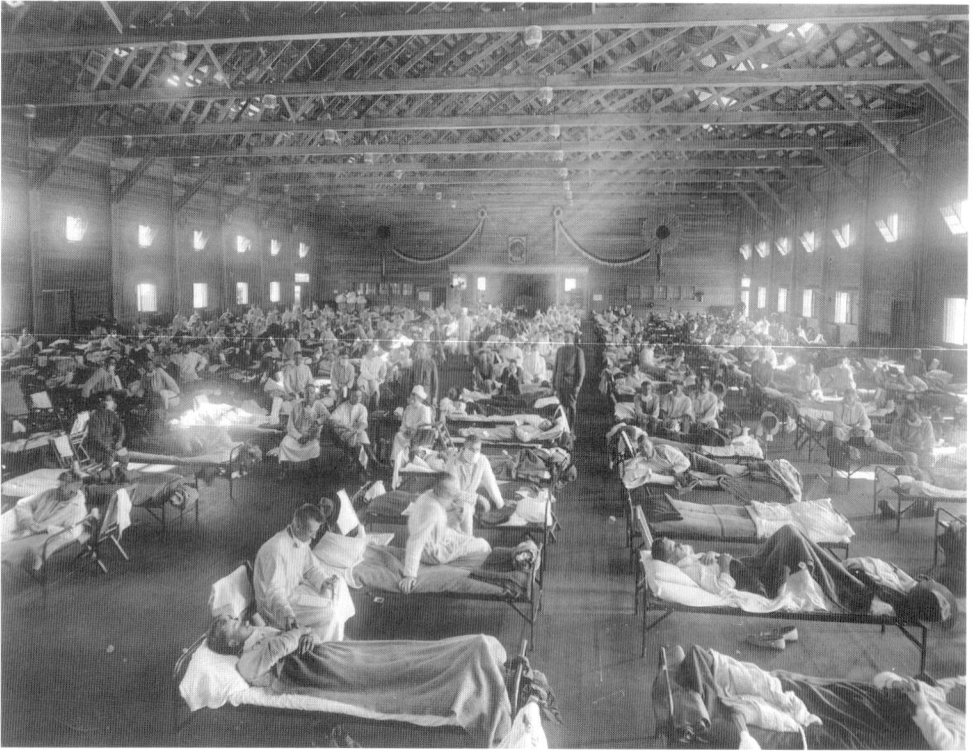

Emergency Spanish flu hospital at Camp Funston, Kansas, 1918, where Albert Gitchell was the first recorded patient in the pandemic. (Public domain image)

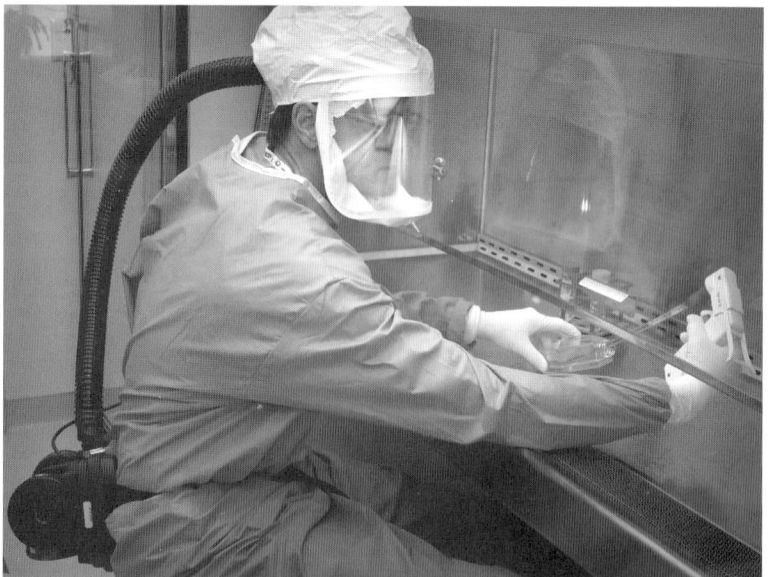

Created in 2005, this photograph depicts one of the Centers for Disease Control's (CDC) staff microbiologists using an electronic pipette to extract reconstructed 1918 Pandemic Influenza virus from a vial containing a supernatant culture medium.

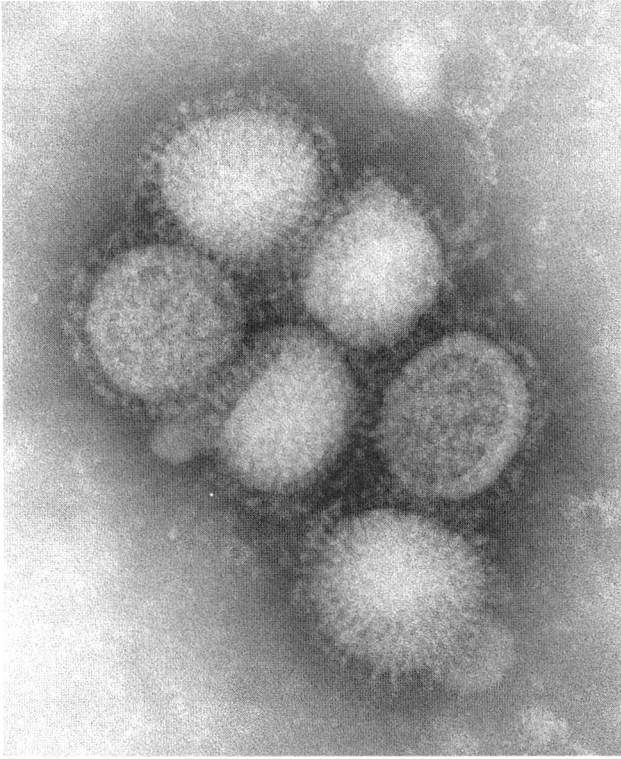
H1N1 Influenza virus. (Wikimedia Commons)

Anenurin Bevan, Minister of Health, on the first day of the National Health Service, 5 July 1948, at Park Hospital, Davyhulme, near Manchester. (Wikimedia Commons)

The first electron microscope, 1933. (Wikimedia Commons)

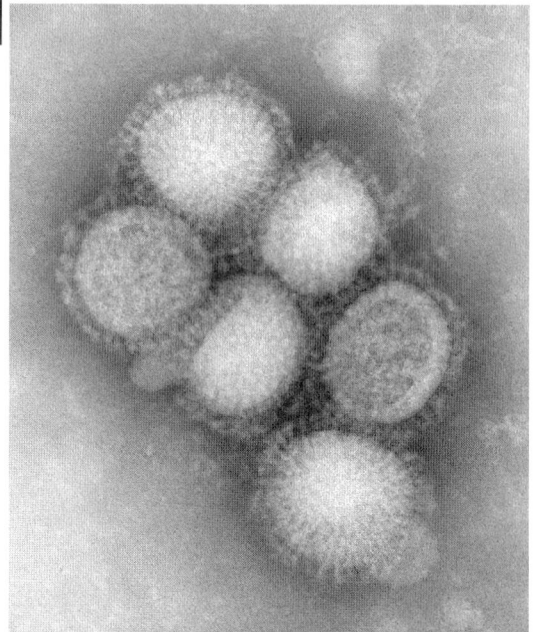

This digitally-colourised, negative-stained transmission electron microscopic (TEM) image depicted some of the ultrastructural morphology of the A/CA/4/09 Swine Flu virus.

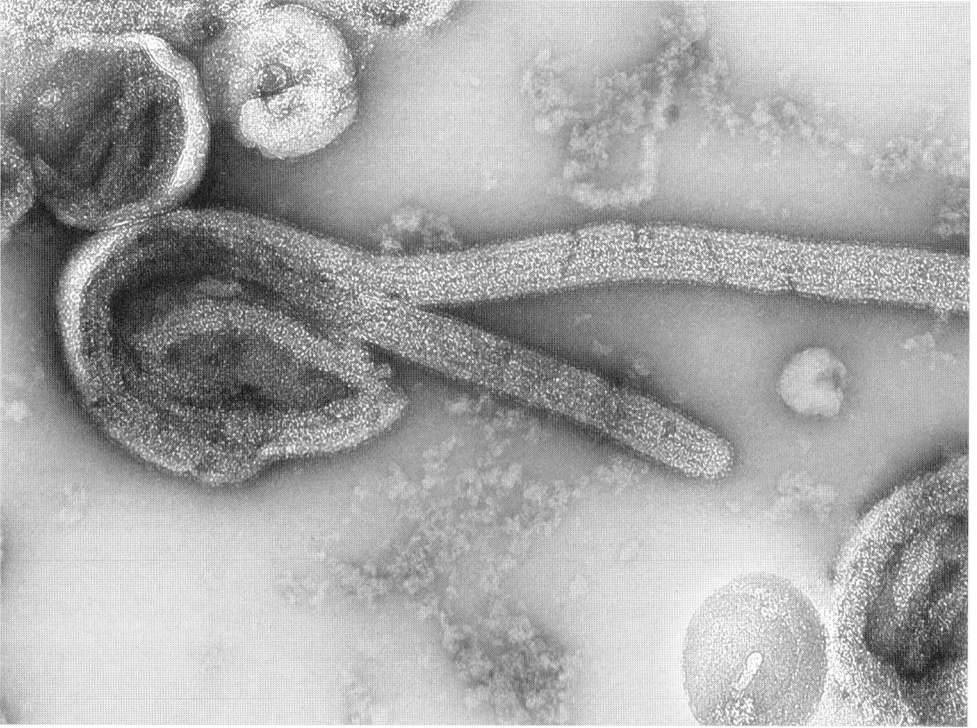

This is an electron microscopic image of the 1976 isolate of Ebola virus. The internal structures of the filamentous particle are visible, including the nucleocapsid and other structural viral proteins, and the outer viral envelope is covered with surface projections. The characteristic '6-shape' of the virus is evident. (Wikimedia Commons)

McDonalds sponsored the Olympics in London in 2012. This is their outlet at the Olympic park. Many argued this associated sport with junk food in a favourable way. (Wikimedia Commons)

A campaign poster from an AIDS
conference in Durban, South Africa, in
2016, highlighting the plight of HIV
patients who can't afford the medication.
(Wikimedia Commons)

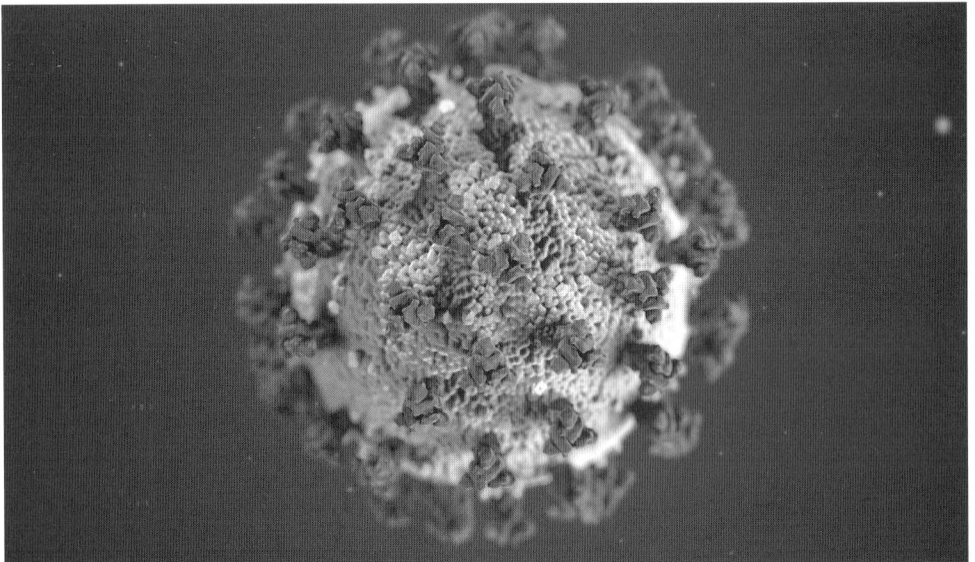

This illustration, created at the Centers for Disease Control and Prevention (CDC), reveals ultra
structural morphology exhibited by coronaviruses. Note the spikes that adorn the outer surface of the
virus, which impart the look of a corona surrounding the virion, when viewed electron microscopically.
A novel coronavirus, named Severe Acute Respiratory Syndrome coronavirus 2 (SARS-CoV-2), was
identified as the cause of an outbreak of respiratory illness first detected in Wuhan, China in 2019. The
illness caused by this virus has been named coronavirus disease 2019 (COVID-19).

Russian mural during Covid-19 pandemic. (Anton Maksimov)

An example of a Covid ad in the UK. (Wikimedia Commons)

Pro-NHS mural, UK, 2020. (Edward Howell)

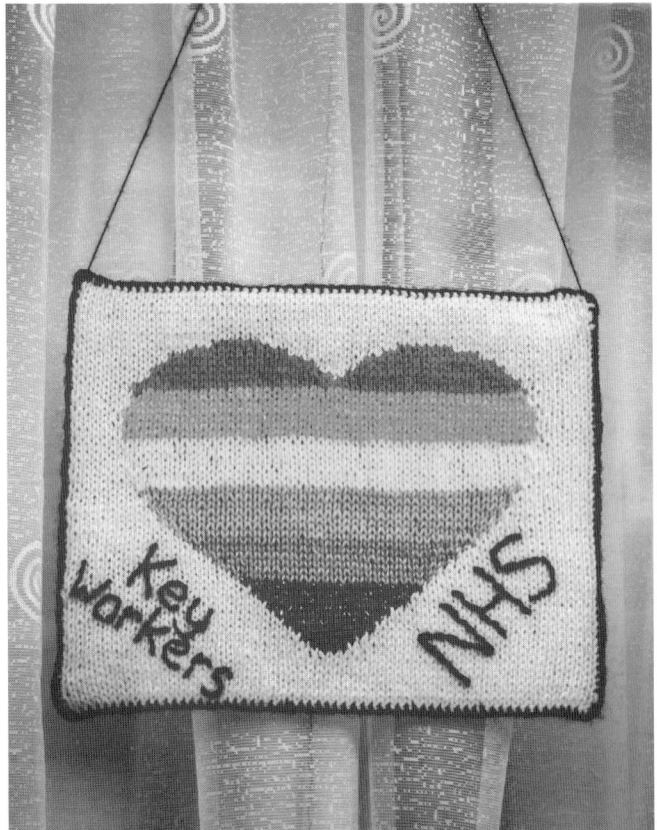

During 2020 people hung
pictures in their windows
thanking the NHS.
(K. Mitch Hodge)

fact that, according to the book *The Fourth Revolution: The Global Race to Reinvent the State*, it was translated in to twenty-two languages and copies of it were dropped from planes across Germany as a form of pro-British propaganda. (Two copies were actually found in Hitler's bunker). The war made increased state involvement in private life a matter of patriotism and civic duty, and by its end the people of Britain had come to accept the government's presence in the minutiae of their lives through things like rationing programmes, the Home Guard and the evacuation programme. It is hard to imagine a society readily allowing its government to prescribe what to eat, or allowing their children to be sent away in any other circumstances. This softening to state involvement in private life, coupled with the change in mood among intellectuals from eugenics to strengthening society by provision, meant the welfare reforms proposed by Clement Atlee's government after 1945 were welcomed largely with open arms by the population.

Nye Bevan's vision for the NHS was supported off the back other major reforms recommended by the Beveridge Report, including universal free secondary education, family allowance payments to help those with children, the National Assistance Act which aimed to care for those in need due to age or disability, and the National Insurance Act which improved the method of taxation that would ultimately pay for the changes. Social housing had existed since 1919, but a new post-war building programme aimed not just to create new homes for council tenants, but to create entire new towns with good services where the needs of different stratas of society – school, work, transport, healthcare, recreation – could all be met.

But the NHS and associated welfare state reforms were not completely without opposition. Political Historian Anthony Broxton says Churchill described Bevan as 'a windbag and a dreamer',[3] and worried that he, along with some other Labour MPs, were looking to subvert the coalition government. In 1946, when Nye Bevan, now Health Minister in the newly elected post-war Labour government, published his bill on the health service, Broxton says a former chairman of the British Medical Association described it as the first step toward 'National Socialism as practiced in Germany'. The BMA spent the next two years campaigning against the terms offered for doctors, which resulted in the freedom to continue to run private practices as well as work for the state. Even so, in

1948, the BMA claimed only 10 per cent of their members supported the creation of the NHS. The Tory opposition, perhaps still bitter at the loss of the election only two months after Nazi surrender, repeatedly voted against the bill to implement the NHS. Ultimately, though, the National Health Service Act finally carried by 337 votes to 178.

The National Health Service took control of 480,000 hospital beds, 125,000 nurses and 5,000 consultants on 5 July 1948. It did not increase or improve resources at that time, it just changed how it was organised, paid for and accessed. It divided the existing stock of hospitals and clinics – and those who worked for them – into fourteen regional hospital boards, thirty-six boards of governors for teaching hospitals, 388 hospital management committees, 138 executive councils, and 147 local health authorities.

A major casualty of the NHS were the Friendly and Mutual Aid societies, like the one in Bevan's beloved Tredegar. Many other countries had used National Health Insurance-style legislation to scale up cover provided by such organisations, but in the UK, they largely became redundant. Before the Second World War, Friendly Societies were a good example of workers self-organising, and of communities rallying around through fundraising activities like fetes. The control of Friendly Societies always remained with the members and they were a focal point for local people. Although the support they offered did not extend to everyone, and was patchy in terms of what was supplied town to town, not everyone was happy to see those societies replaced by a state-run system in which they had little or no say. In fact, one of the biggest supporters of the Friendly Societies was actually William Beveridge. Having previously recommended universal public health care and welfare provided by the state in his ground-breaking report, he appears to have rounded on his own ideas later on.

In 1948, Beveridge authored the book *Voluntary Action*, a work that defends the role of mutual aid groups in the provision of services like healthcare and recommends that state provision does not step on the toes of those seeking to provide more for themselves than just the minimum. He said he believed voluntary action, for bettering yourself and others, was a 'distinguishing mark of a free society'.[4] It can sometimes be hard to distinguish between Beveridge's reputation as an instrument of the Left with his own, liberal political leanings. But while this third report seeks to justify the existence of the private sector, particularly when it comes to healthcare provision, it appears he meant the two systems to coexist, with the private sector acting as a buffer to state provision as a tool for social equity.

In the shadow of the NHS, many friendly organisations simply disappeared – especially those whose main purpose was to provide access to healthcare. Many of them had been struggling with waning membership and involvement already, thanks to the war. However, others refined their role away from their grass roots organisational framework, into a more regulated service, mostly offering financial or insurance products for members. Some 200 friendly societies exist today, and are still part of our daily life. The Co-Op, for example, was essentially a food bank launched in 1844 in Rochdale. It offered access to affordable produce for members and anyone could join. Later it began offering banking services to help finance its core food-related activities and a dividend pay-out for members. Credit unions, building societies, and mutual aid societies all have their roots in the original Friendly Society movement. The Tredegar Mutual Aid society was finally wound down in 1994. It had just 114 members by then, who received 18p a week to help with their medical costs.

The years of austerity after the Second World War, essential to pay off war debts, sat at odds with the spend required by the new welfare state. Food rationing continued, fuel remained scarce, the pound dropped in value, and there was a significant shortage of housing. In his book *From Cradle To Grave, Fifty Years of the NHS*, author Geoffrey Rivett says, 'It was a long-standing socialist belief that a state medical service would save money.' It had in fact been one of the justifications for the NHS, that good health provision would reduce case load, and keep the population in optimum health to be able to work. But in reality, a universal public health service does not necessarily save money because its priority is developing better practices, new treatments and saving lives. The estimated annual cost in 1946 was £110 million. By 1951, the actual cost had ballooned to £384 million and how to pay for it was of great concern to the government. Rivett says, 'It seemed virtually certain that the increasing outlay as medical science progressed would be more and more "uneconomic" … Medicine was buying life at an ever-increasing marginal cost.'

I think the vast-majority of people would agree that they wouldn't want it any other way, but it presented a series of new problems to this service that needed to be addressed quickly, efficiently and creatively. One of those issues was public mind-set. Rivett suggests that the 'illusion they were getting something for nothing' resulted in people using the NHS for free medical supplies like aspirin and laxatives – things they would previously have paid for. Instead of an education campaign to help people understand that the NHS was not limitless, and that everyone paid for its use, the Chancellor Hugh Gaitskell proposed legislation that made it possible to charge for things like glasses and dentures. Bevan resigned from his role in protest in 1951. He felt the government could have done more to level out the tax burden on different social classes, and he did not agree with charges for healthcare at any level. When the Conservative government won the election later that year, they introduced a prescription charge. In 1953, the government appointed a committee to review the NHS, chaired by economist Claude Guillbaud. When the report was published, it was found that the actual figures, when adjusted for inflation, showed the cost of the NHS was in fact falling, in real terms.

Another major issue for the early NHS was staffing. While the training of doctors was managed and numbers capped by the state, no provision for the training of nurses had been included in legislation and nobody had responsibility for it. This meant there were serious shortages of nurses right from the outset. Rivett says the NHS was estimated to have a nursing shortfall of 48,000 almost immediately, and relied on untrained and/or unskilled staff. For the solution, Britain looked to its former Empire.

A month before the official launch of the NHS, the ship *Empire Windrush* arrived at Tilbury docks. On board were almost 500 workers from the Caribbean, here to help rebuild Britain after the war. Thousands of new workers arrived each year and by 1961, there were 161,000 immigrants, mostly from the Caribbean, in England and Wales to even out the deficit between able-bodied workers and jobs. A large proportion of the women migrants found work as nurses, and nursing aides in the newly formed NHS. By 1955 there were NHS recruitment centres set up in places like Barbados to attract qualified nurses to the UK. Without their contribution, the NHS would have struggled to fulfil its mandate. It simply could not meet the needs of the population from the pool of

British staff available, especially as many British women returned to their primary role of homemaker after the war. Reliance on migrant workers has been essential ever since. Additional changes to the way nurses were trained, and the influence they had in directing healthcare policy, also improved their working conditions and attracted more people to the profession in the long term.

Among the many crises of the early years of the NHS, one of the most acute was relating to General Practice. GPs had traditionally operated as one-man-bands, usually seeing patients at home or from an office in their own house. They saw the number of patients double between 1948 and 1950 under the NHS, but the amount they were paid to see a patient did not cover additional work, such as administration, booking appointments, cleaning, answering the phone – basically, GPs did not have the army of support staff we are used to seeing today, they did everything themselves, and they weren't happy about it.

Unlike hospital consultants and surgeons, GPs did not work for the NHS but rather were contractors who had signed up to supply a service. This was one of the concessions they had won from Bevan in the months before the NHS launched. By 1966, GPs were threatening a mass resignation from the NHS and a return to private practice, and the government had to act. In 1966, the Family Doctor Charter was agreed, which allowed GPs to claim all their premises costs and 70 per cent of the cost of employing support staff. There were also financial incentives for forming a 'group' with three or more GPs, the basis of the local model we are used to today, and additional payment for out of hours' services and professional development. This resulted in the professionalisation of general practice, and the start of the group-run, multi-service, purpose-built clinics common in the twenty-first century.

In its first twenty years, the NHS had to deal with some major events. The treatment of communicable disease, such as smallpox and TB, gave way to more lifestyle-based chronic diseases. Smallpox, for example, had been brought under control by a global vaccine programme delivered in conjunction with the World Health Organisation, but the threat from smoking-related diseases was increasing. In 1960, more than 60 per cent of men in the UK smoked, and the mortality rate for lung cancer was high. The NHS could no longer rely on simply treating people as they had done with communicable disease. They had to find new drugs to fight cancer, and they had to embark on an education programme to promote lifestyle change in the at-risk population. It was a huge swerve for the service.

Screening services for disease with good treatment programmes available were launched. However, for diseases where there was limited chance of a good outcome the need for early detection was seen as less of a priority. The expansion of specialised services to help patients with more easily treatable conditions saw a huge growth in the number of consultants, and a reorganisation of hospitals into clear clinical divisions. Meanwhile, the role of those working on drug development for those diseases with less than effective treatments was also expanding. Synthetic penicillin was manufactured for the first time by Surrey-based pharmaceutical group Beecham Laboratories, and the discovery of chlorothiazide, an oral diuretic, revolutionised treatment for heart disease.

The Family Planning Association spearheaded clinical trials of oral contraceptives and by 1968 around one million British women were using them regularly. Meanwhile, three different inventions by Harold Hopkins from Imperial College London made the endoscopy process much easier and more comfortable, and paved the way for minimally invasive surgical techniques. GPs also began to use vaccines, like the one for measles, as a preventative measure. It reduced the number of children who contracted this seasonal disease, reducing GP workload and the prescribing of antibiotics – which was closely monitored by government. Other diseases like Polio, which increased the long-term burden on the NHS through disability and reduced the quality of life of the victim, were now preventable through the vaccination programme.

The health service was changing as the challenges being presented by society also changed. The population had increased, but standards of living were better. The NHS had better tools to fight acute and infectious diseases, but more focus needed to be placed on chronic and degenerative diseases. Other lifestyle changes, like the increase in motor vehicles and the emergence of music festivals, also needed to be considered in the healthcare context. Technological advancement in both equipment and medicine development was increasingly more rapid. It was time for a restructure.

Over the next decade, much more focus was placed on general health and wellbeing, and the prevention of lifestyle-based diseases. Those working within the NHS turned their attention to quality of care, and how to guarantee the same, predictable standards UK-wide. More than one audit had shown up regional variations in care and outcomes, as well as differing care standards experienced by patients across different conditions. Sometimes it wasn't easy to pinpoint why the results were so varied. Perhaps the most well-known report of the era was the Seebohm Report, which recommended the integration of children, elderly and mental welfare services into one department in each local authority. For the first time, social services and healthcare were separated – a separation that still exists. Meanwhile, social security and healthcare were united in one government department.

Proposals for a complete restructure of the way the NHS was managed kept being written and stalled, with the public flip-flopping between governments at the general election resulting in further revisions and delays. A 1968 Green Paper on the NHS commissioned by the Labour administration was subjected to two significant rewrites under Edward Heath's Conservative government sworn in, in 1970. Eventually, in 1973, the service was placed under the control of ninety newly created local health authorities, just before Labour were re-elected.

The focus on local provision of healthcare rather than Bevan's centralised model, which was discounted by Bevan and Atlee originally due to fears of future Conservative governments cutting funding and blaming local authorities for the fall out, became more acute under the Thatcher administration. Industrial action in the early 1980s by NHS staff led to accusations from Thatcher that patients were being put at risk, while the concerns of staff over training, pay and safe working environments went unaddressed. A further restructure in 1984 aimed to reduce bureaucratic tiers – and the cost of them – and make the service more flexible to regional characteristics, while also introducing a non-medical general management level and reducing the overall number of staff. But doctors worried about their clinical freedoms, concerned that pen-pushers might make cost-saving decisions that could put patients at risk. Meanwhile, the Royal College of Nursing continued to protest the lack of nurses involved at management-level decision making.

During the Thatcher years, the process of tendering out for services was also established, allowing private contractors to take up roles and provide goods within the previously closed loop of the NHS, which also did not sit well with clinical staff. The same medical profession that once fought against Nye Bevan's NHS plans, now took ownership of the service and began defending it as their own.

The 1980s saw the battleground drawn up on which future public healthcare provision would be fought for, and by whom. But while medical staff and bureaucrats argued over who controlled budgets, the honeymoon period from communicable diseases was coming to an end. The NHS was about to fight a whole series of new battles that were predominantly medical in nature. The new age of pandemics had arrived.

Chapter VIII

Smallpox and the Greater Good – the Story of Vaccines

'I hope that someday the practice of producing cowpox in human beings will spread over the world – when that day comes, there will be no more smallpox.'

Edward Jenner

In September 1978, Reg Wickett was on holiday with his wife in Dorset. An engineer at Birmingham City Hospital, he almost had to cancel his long-awaited beach break. Just the week before, a young woman called Janet Parker had been taken seriously ill and admitted to hospital. It appeared she had contracted smallpox.

Thought to have been eradicated from the wild completely for over a year, and not endemic in the UK for decades, the terrifying resurgence of this deadly disease was not taken lightly by authorities. Janet also worked at the hospital as an anatomy photographer, and as she lay in bed in an isolation ward at the specialist Catherine-de-Barnes hospital, an investigation was under way to trace the source of her illness. All the staff at the hospital were offered an emergency vaccination, and Reg was one of hundreds who queued diligently for hours to receive a jab in both arms, before heading off with his wife.

But just days into his vacation, the authorities tracked him down and made him return to Birmingham. Apparently, the diagnosis of smallpox had been confirmed and more jabs were necessary but no one knew where Reg had gone. A massive appeal had been launched to trace him. He was given two further jabs, but fell gravely ill. He ended up in the Catherine-de-Barnes hospital alongside Janet.

Decades later he spoke to the *Birmingham Mail* about his experience.

I was having hallucinations, I was dreaming, having nightmares. I couldn't keep my eyes open. They were pumping stuff into me, giving me tablets every ten minutes and it was a terrible couple of days. They told me afterwards it was cowpox that I had. Because that was what was used to combat smallpox. It's got some of the same symptoms as smallpox.

Sadly, Janet died on 11 September 1978 after catching pneumonia. Her case was linked to Professor Henry Bedson, a virologist at the hospital who had been studying smallpox. He was so devastated by what had happened that he took his own life. Across Birmingham, 260 people were quarantined in their own home. Holidays were cancelled, weddings postponed, but thankfully there were no further deaths. Across the globe, the WHO arranged for smallpox samples to be destroyed – today there are only two left for research purposes, in high security units in America and Russia.

This is the story of the last known case of smallpox. It is tragic, and terrifying. But only a few years later the Catherine-de-Barnes hospital had been developed in to luxury homes, and smallpox was a thing of the past. A worldwide vaccination programme had killed off the disease completely, the dream of any epidemiologist. It was simply gone. The total eradication of smallpox was the end of a process starting over 200 years before, with Edward Jenner and cowpox – the thing that almost killed Reg Wickett.

Smallpox was one of the world's oldest diseases, believed to have appeared in humans around 10,000 BC alongside agriculture. It spread through the globe with merchants, becoming epidemic in new populations, then endemic. It seems to have been present at the end of the Bronze Age, was responsible for the Antonine plague which heralded the fall of Rome. It destroyed the ancient American civilisations of the Aztecs and Incas, and almost wiped out the first nations' people of North America. It is the ultimate bad guy.

Caused by the variola virus – from the Latin word 'varius', meaning 'stained' – it became known as 'small pockes' in the fifteenth century, the word 'pockes' meaning sack. This referred to the lesions or marks that generally covered the body of those infected. Sometimes it was also called the 'Speckled Monster'. Of course, viruses weren't even theorised until the end of the nineteenth century, so no one knew the exact cause of the disease. But as early as 430 BC it was understood that if you survived it you were immune for life.

In Africa, India and China the practice of variolation developed to try and prevent people from developing the full-blown disease. This involved taking a sharp object, lancing a pocke to cover the object in infected pus, and then applying that to superficial scratches in the skin of the uninfected. The hope was that the recipient would receive a low-level, protective case of the disease.

By the eighteenth century, 400,000 Europeans a year were dying of smallpox,[1] and if you lived you had lifelong disfiguring scars and a one in three chance of going blind. In London's children, the death rate was about 80 per cent. It really was the absolute scourge of the time. The practice of variolation arrived in England in 1721, and spread rapidly despite the risks involved – you could still catch smallpox or spread the disease to others who were not immune.

In 1757, 8-year-old Edward Jenner received variolation in Gloucester. He developed a strong interest in science and medicine and at age 13 began an apprenticeship to a country surgeon near Bristol. One day he claimed to have heard a milkmaid say that she would never get smallpox because she had already had cowpox – a milder disease common in the farming community. Jenner eventually went to work at St George's Hospital in London around 1770, where he heard further tales of those who worked closely with cows being immune to smallpox, something that seemed to be common knowledge in the farming community.

Jenner wondered if smallpox variolation could be replaced with cowpox, conferring immunity with less risk. In 1796, he tested the theory by taking some of the fresh, infectious material from a cowpox sufferer and using it to variolate an 8-year-old boy, James Phipps. He was mildly unwell for ten days and then recovered. Two months later, Jenner infected the boy with smallpox, but no disease developed. Pushing the shocking ethics of that experiment aside for a moment, he had proven his new low risk inoculation method worked. He called it vaccination after the Latin name for cowpox – vaccinia.

Jenner immediately sent a letter to the Royal Society but they rejected his experiment. So, he undertook more trials and in 1798 he published a small booklet about his work called, *An Inquiry into the Causes and Effects of the Variolae Vaccinae, a disease discovered in some of the western counties of England, particularly Gloucestershire and Known by the Name of Cow Pox.* Although not exactly greeted with universal praise at first, the use of

Jenner's inoculation against smallpox began to spread and by 1800 it was common across Europe. Later that year the vaccine arrived in America and President Thomas Jefferson was so impressed he set up a National Vaccine Institute to start a programme.

Jenner devoted his entire life to promoting the method of vaccination. But he never sought to make money from it, and used to vaccinate the poor from his home for free. Nevertheless, he was the recipient of many great honours, apparently even respected by Napoleon despite being British. But he was also the victim of attacks and ridicule. By the end of his life in 1820 he was borderline reclusive, although still working. Often referred to as the creator or father of vaccination, Stefan Riedal MD[2] rather suggests he is the father of the controlled, scientific process of inoculation. He said in a paper in 2005, 'It was his relentless promotion and devoted research of vaccination that changed the way medicine was practiced.' He took something precarious, and made it safe and with a uniform outcome. Now the goal was to do this for other diseases.

Before Jenner died, two amazing things happened. Firstly, the figures for deaths from smallpox released in 1820 showed a decrease of almost two thirds since Jenner's inoculation programme began, bolstering the new industry created around vaccines. Secondly, Jenner realised that vaccination was not lifelong, and that people would need to be inoculated again as adults.

That second revelation isn't just important for the lives it saved among those who needed a second dose later on. It also changed the direction of vaccine research and allowed the process to start to become more refined. In 1836, early pharmacologist Edward Ballard noted the need to create Jenner's vaccine from new strains of cowpox as the old ones were too 'weak' to work. This led to the deliberate infecting of young calves in order to gather the material needed to manufacture vaccines.[3] In 1850, on the advice of Robert Koch, vaccine producers began to use glycerine to kill bacteria but preserve the lymph – the essential part of the vaccine needed for immunity. The vaccine was now more stable, the supply more constant, and the risk of transmitting other diseases during vaccination had been dramatically reduced. Science was now looking at how that process could be repeated for other diseases that didn't have a naturally weaker version in the wild. That process was centred on understanding bacteria.

In 1625, Galileo Galilei had submitted an invention to the Accademia dei Lincei which he called the 'little eye', but later came to be known as the compound microscope. This was not the first microscope, and although often credited as the inventor, Galileo simply refined an invention based on previous iterations dating back 4,000 years. However, this was the first time the microscope was taken seriously in scientific research. By the 1670s, it was a common piece of equipment for the naturalists and botanists of England. The use soon crossed over in to medicine. In 1676, Antoni van Leeuwenhoek observed microorganisms in water for the first time using a microscope – he had discovered bacteria, and with it the discipline of microbiology. And although smallpox is a virus, and viruses would not be thought about as a separate entity for more than 200 years, microbiology became essential in the development of early vaccines.

Pasteur's work on the attenuation of chicken cholera bacterium in the 1870s turned out to be the next most major advance in vaccinations.[4] Having left a chicken cholera culture exposed to air over a long holiday, he returned to find cholera still present but significantly weakened. He theorised that you could use this weaker strain to inoculate a patient, giving them the protective properties needed without the risk associated with the illness. This would also make it possible to develop vaccines for diseases other than smallpox without having to seek out a natural, weaker strain. We call vaccines that use an artificially weakened version of a disease to promote immunity 'live attenuated' vaccines.

Pasteur then began work on an anthrax vaccine using the same method. At the time, anthrax was devastating farm animal stocks. He proved it worked in a public, controlled experiment in 1881 on sheep and cows. He had shown that safe vaccines could be created and reproduced for other diseases for the first time, using an attenuated version of the disease itself. (Princetown Professor of History, Gerald L. Geison, discovered in the 1990s that Pasteur had lied about the way the vaccine was prepared, and appropriated the work of a rival, little known veterinarian Jean-Joseph Henri Toussaint. However, Geison said Pasteur still deserved his reputation as 'one of the greatest scientists who ever lived'.[5])

In 1885, Pasteur's rabies vaccine based on the same principle was used on a human for the first time with success. Meanwhile in Spain, Jaime Ferrán developed the first human vaccine for cholera – a bacterium only isolated for the first time by Robert Koch the year before. Although

Ferrán's vaccine was controversial and met with mixed results, he went on to develop vaccines against plague, tetanus, typhus, tuberculosis and rabies.

The last half of the nineteenth century was a glory period for what we now call preventative medicine. New diseases were being classified for the first time, such as diphtheria, and the relationship between other diseases like chickenpox and shingles started to be understood. Vaccinations for various bacterial illnesses seemed to be developing at a rate of knots. Although viral vaccinations other than for smallpox were still not possible, science was moving forward with the understanding that viruses existed. During this period, scientists in Western Europe were realising that humans needn't be the victims of disease, running from and fighting potential epidemics. Illnesses that had been problematic for centuries were now being brought under human control thanks to science. It felt like a turning point for humanity, we were finally the masters in the fight against disease. Then in 1900, everything changed.

In June 1894 in Rutland County, Vermont, a number of people began to fall ill. Symptoms included sore throat, fever, exhaustion, headache and stomach pain. In some these symptoms developed into meningitis and paralysis that in some cases stopped the patient breathing. Although it is impossible to know exactly how many people were infected in Rutland, records show 132 cases of permanent paralysis, and eighteen deaths. This was the first major outbreak of poliomyelitis, and it would once again alter the direction of medical science. By 1900 there were thousands of cases each year, usually in clusters.

Polio is another ancient disease – although it is not zoonotic – with its effects shown in Egyptian carvings dating back to 1400 BC. It was first clinically described by an English physician, Michael Underwood, in 1789. It later became known as Heine-Medin disease after two prominent physicians who studied it, and then infantile paralysis. Until 1900 it was not an epidemic disease. There might be small outbreaks here and there, but always limited to a few, young children. For that reason, people didn't think it was contagious. Even in Rutland it wasn't considered communicable – in some families a child died while others appeared to not even be ill.

This 'infantile paralysis' became increasingly more common in the early years of the twentieth century, with clusters of infections across

Europe and America causing the death or long-term disability of many children. Science began to turn its attention to this problem.

In 1905, Swedish doctor Ivar Wickman studied a series of outbreaks in Scandinavia, and realised the disease was contained in spinal fluid. The following year, Austrian medical duo Karl Landsteiner and Erwin Popper put some infected spinal fluid through a bacterial filter, and then used the fluid to infect monkeys who became ill with polio. They concluded it must be a virus – which had only been proven to exist sixteen years before – because the filter would otherwise have stopped bacteria from passing through. The hypothesised 'virus' was known to be smaller and able to pass through these filters. They came up with the name poliomyelitis, which means inflammation of the spinal cord.

Now we knew polio was communicable, but there was no treatment. Viruses would not be seen by the human eye for another thirty years, after the invention of the electron microscope. The lack of understanding around viruses meant there was no hope of a vaccination. Large outbreaks began to erupt through the developed world – in 1916 in the USA there were 27,000 cases and 6,000 deaths. In the UK, almost 8,000 children a year were paralysed by polio, and around 700 died. Polio would strike in the summer each year, affecting mostly children aged 5 to 9. It closed cinemas and public swimming pools, it terrified parents and was utterly devastating – a new plague.

We now understand that our increased living standards, and the decline of other bacterial diseases through medical advances, contributed to epidemic polio. Through most of human history, children had been exposed to the polio virus while they were still babes in arms, with protection from their mother's immune system resulting in 'natural vaccination'. But by 1900, cleaner homes, access to purer water, and a reduction in infant breastfeeding all meant this exposure to polio was delayed until children were older, and/or without their mother's immunity to help them.

In the absence of a vaccine, or any real treatment, a system needed to be developed to care for polio patients. In the first-half of the twentieth century this was haphazard, with health workers often removing from their families children whom they thought might be infected and isolating them in hospitals. The invention of the assisted breathing machine, the Iron Lung, by American Philip Drinker in 1928 meant many more lives could be saved – but these came at a cost. Patients could be required, on average, to spend two weeks in an Iron Lung while they recovered. Hospitals now had to invest in a large number of these machines – and places to put them. For some patients, ongoing use of the Iron Lung was needed, especially at night – which meant a protracted hospital stay.

Then 1952 happened. It was one of the worst pandemic years for polio in the Western world. In Copenhagen, at the Blegdamshospitalet, they expected a few hundred cases each summer, but reached capacity within the first few weeks. Over nineteen weeks they saw 2,700 patients – and 316 of those could not breathe. But Denmark had only one Iron Lung in the entire country[6] and they had no idea how they were going to manage. Luckily, a member of the medical team called Mogens Bjørneboe had seen a college use an alternative method to support breathing on a tetanus patient just a few months before. When faced with a child too young for an Iron Lung, anaesthetist Bjørn Ibsen had used positive pressure ventilation – a tube was inserted into the child's windpipe and a member of staff squeezed a rubber balloon to help them breathe. Previously used just for short periods during surgery, this child had been ventilated by a team working in shifts for two weeks.

With a combination of anaesthesia and hand ventilation, Ibsen saved the life of a 12-year-old girl who doctors had thought was in the terminal phase of the disease. Suddenly it was all hands-on deck. Each patient needed a team of four people to work the ventilation in shifts, and they may have required that support for several months. Swathes of medical students were mobilised to support trained staff, and Denmark's Polio death rate dropped by 70 per cent. The following year, the company Engström in neighbouring Sweden invented a machine to mechanically pump the air. This was the birth of intensive care. Although a vaccination for Polio became available in 1955, the benefits of intensive care for a wide variety of patients meant that this type of treatment on specialist wards quickly became a feature of most European hospitals. Once again, medicine responded to a problem in a way that would shift the human expectation of what is possible, and where treatment could, or should, draw the line.

The inventor of the polio vaccine was an American called Jonas Salk. His work was funded by a national charity called the National Institute for Infant Paralysis, which today is known as the March of Dimes.

Founded by President Roosevelt, himself partially paralysed thanks to polio, the National Institute for Infant Paralysis was funded by a new, social-giving model. Instead of seeking out one or two large donors from among industry or the super-rich, Roosevelt asked American people to send dimes to the White House to fund its work. Not only was this model successful financially, but it changed the way the American people thought about philanthropy.

Charitable giving had previously been based on the European model of the rich giving to the poor (to save their souls or later, for notoriety). Roosevelt might not like the use of this word, but he effectively 'socialised' charitable giving – making the process of gifting very small amounts acceptable, and encouraging the public to work together by pooling small gifts for a collective end, rather than one large donor being celebrated. This is a model that still underpins the public donation and fundraising model of charitable giving today – think of Captain Tom Moore's walk to support the NHS charities during the Covid pandemic.

Salk was working in a team, that was one of many teams focused on a polio vaccine. The leading idea, proposed by Albert Sabin, was based on Pasteur's live attenuated virus model. But Salk had another idea that involved killing and preserving the virus, as followers of Koch had done with the cowpox variolation 100 years before. A massive human trial showed the vaccine worked, and five companies were licensed to produce the vaccine – Salk himself refused a patent for his work, saying the vaccine belonged to the people.

In the UK, the advent of a polio vaccine once again changed the landscape of healthcare. Although Edward Jenner had birthed the modern concept of vaccination in the UK, the government had been slow on the uptake of other vaccinations when they became available. Only smallpox had been offered routinely, with a diphtheria vaccination programme starting during the Second World War. But the British public now demanded polio vaccination as standard.[7] The polio vaccination programme launched in 1956 in the UK and was initially focused on priority groups. But the British public, who at the time had a huge sense of ownership over their newly formed NHS, wanted more from the government. They demanded that all children receive the polio vaccine, and that this be an ongoing programme of protection, not just one launched during outbreaks.

This was initially problematic for the British government, because of issues with supply. Due to an incident in the US where some vaccines had not been prepared correctly and had caused polio outbreaks, the UK had decided to manufacture its own with additional rigorous tests. This slowed manufacture down, and at first only two doses were being given rather than the recommended three. Some local authorities were unwilling to introduce vaccine programmes at all until the supply was secure. But the British public and the media were not happy about this situation and the government came under fire. Even the *British Medical Journal* ran an editorial criticising the government's approach to managing expectations, admonishing them for trying to win over public opinion rather than focusing on good health policy.[8]

The polio vaccine was seen as a rational choice and a universal right by the British public and under elevated pressure the government eventually agreed to import the Salk vaccine. Now registration was required to make sure demand could be met, and clear records of who had the vaccine and how many doses were being kept. The polio vaccination model started a national, ongoing vaccine campaign that would form the basis of the routine vaccination programme enjoyed by the British public today.

Back in the US, Sabin initially discarded his rival vaccine, but in 1957 the WHO decided to test that one further. Tests showed it was safe, and by the mid-1960 it had replaced Salk's vaccine and become the most commonly used version. It was faster and cheaper to produce, and did not require a trained health worker to administer it, speeding up vaccination programmes worldwide. For the WHO, this also meant they could partner with local agencies in developing countries. Studies have shown uptake increases when local people are involved in the process. It was also a much more pleasant process for the patient, who simply had to eat a sugar cube laced with the vaccine, rather than be jabbed with a needle.

But as soon as Sabin's vaccine, known as OPV (Oral Polio Vaccine) began being used en-masse, there were mysterious outbreaks of polio, cases of paralysis, and even a few deaths. Although the medical community initially defended the OPV, research in the 1980s showed that the live virus in the OPV can mutate inside the intestinal tract, putting the recipient and people close to them at risk of a more virulent form of the virus. The risk was considered low, and most countries continued to use the OPV because it was easier and uptake was higher. But by 1994, most of the Western world had eliminated wild polio completely. The risk of reintroducing it back in to the population through OPV was too great, and since the year 2000 most of Europe and America have used the original vaccine developed by Salk.

Around the time the link between polio outbreaks and the vaccine were discovered in the early 1980s, there was a temporary drop in uptake of the vaccine as parents lost their trust in it. A huge education and vaccination campaign was launched by WHO in 1988 to try and wipe out polio completely. Today, there are only two countries in the world that still have endemic polio – Afghanistan and Pakistan. But while polio is on track to become the second disease in history to be wiped out by an international vaccination programme, vaccine scepticism persists in every country in the world.

Vaccine sceptics – or anti-vaxxers as they're more commonly known – have existed for as long as vaccines themselves. In 1853, smallpox vaccinations were made mandatory in England and in 1867 penalties for vaccine refusal were added. The outcry was palpable. But Many people resisted, stating that they had rights to liberty over their own body and that of their children. The National Anti-Vaccination League was formed in 1866 in London, originally to fight the compulsory nature of the smallpox vaccine. Much of the fear of vaccination at that time stemmed from the cross infection that was a common side effect from the earlier variolation. Others felt vaccinations were ungodly and some decried them for the cruel way they were tested on animals (in 1875 the Victoria Street Society – now known as the National Anti-Vivisection Society – was founded in London by Frances Power Cobbe). In 1907, despite the marked decrease in smallpox, the government agreed to repeal the compulsory nature of the smallpox vaccine for 'conscientious objectors' – and have never attempted to make a vaccine compulsory since. Thankfully the uptake of the smallpox vaccine was high enough that by the 1930s it ceased to be endemic, with the last major outbreak in 1962. However, it was apparent that the miracle of vaccination alone was not enough – medicine had to win hearts as well as minds, and this is what the WHO set out to achieve when they began their smallpox global eradication programme in 1959.

Perhaps one of the most powerful legacies of Edward Jenner is his focus on community practice. Whether this was an intentional ethic, or whether he just didn't like to travel isn't clear. He had, in his younger years, been invited on Captain James Cook's second voyage after helping him catalogue some finds from the first. But Jenner declined. He always practiced in his local community, and this is the model for the smallpox vaccination programme used by the WHO. Jenner also passionately felt vaccines should be free and available to everyone regardless of their geographical area or political divides. In order to achieve that he would teach anyone who was interested how to vaccinate – again, this became part of the model used by the World Health Organisation 150 years later.

When the WHO was created in 1948, the same year the NHS was born, their original priorities were to coordinate healthcare practices and improve outcomes for the United Nations countries. It soon became apparent that, for communicable disease, a global approach was necessary. In order to be successful with their vaccination programmes – starting with smallpox – they partnered with local agencies and trained local people to deliver the vaccines. These groups know their own communities best, can win trust and provide advice and support that is culturally relevant and easy to understand.

This practice has not been without its setbacks. In 1996, Nelson Mandela launched the 'Kick Polio Out of Africa' campaign, along with the WHO's Global Polio Eradication Initiative and Rotary International, an ambitious programme that aimed to vaccinate 50 million children in one year alone. It was a huge success and by 2003, they were on the final stretch with a goal of 15 million children in West and Central Africa. But their efforts were thwarted when religious leaders in Nigeria told parents not to let their children be vaccinated. They believed the polio vaccine was part of a programme of Western genocide against African Muslim people, and that the vaccines contained HIV and would also sterilise young girls.

In a paper in the journal PLoS published in 2007,[9] Ayodele Samiel Jegede argues the context of this belief goes all the way back to the early 1980s, when President Babangida placed a limit of four children on each woman. Immunisation campaigns were being launched at the time and in the psyche of the people the two became connected. In a country where access to medical care was expensive and hard to come by, free vaccinations seemed too good to be true. In addition, the new, democratic, government promoting vaccination was in the Christian south of Nigeria, formerly a

British colony, while the north of the country – where vaccine refusal was highest – was strongly Islamic with a history of resisting colonial rule. Against the backdrop of the events of 11 September 2001, and the war in Iraq, the Muslim people of Nigeria were especially sceptical. A court case against pharmaceutical giant Pfizer, from a 1996 vaccine trial that resulted in several deaths of children, was also still active.

The vaccination programme was halted for almost a year, and polio rose by 30 per cent in the region. The deadlock was eventually broken with diplomacy, but in 2007 an outbreak of vaccine-derived polio, from the live attenuated oral doses commonly used in Africa, created more suspicion and again reduced uptake. It was only in 2020 that Nigeria was finally declared wild polio free. But Afghanistan and Pakistan, where polio is still endemic, continue to struggle with public trust – and sometimes for very good reason.

In 2011, it was discovered that the CIA had posed as agents of a Hepatitis B vaccination programme to gain access to a town where they believed Osama Bin Laden was in hiding. In the past, health workers had been able to gain access to Bin Laden's compound to administer polio drops. An article in the *Scientific American* in May 2013, said, 'The effort apparently failed, but the violation of trust threatens to set back global public health efforts by decades.' Legitimate healthcare workers were chased away from villages, and in Taliban-controlled areas vaccines were completely banned. In 2012, nine people working with the vaccine programme were murdered. During the Covid-19 pandemic, Pakistan's polio programme received further setbacks when villages were too afraid to admit teams with international workers, in case they were carrying coronavirus.

Vaccine scepticism in Europe and America often carries similar undertones of fear of government. The difference is that the people avoiding vaccines are usually afraid of their own government. While it is easy to write off vaccine scepticism as part of the dark world of QAnon conspiracy theories, the roots of that fear are often based in disturbing fact. For example, when the smallpox vaccine first arrived in America, Thomas Jefferson – then an amateur scientist and not yet the president – chose to test it out on three black slaves. In 1932, the Tuskegee Institute in Alabama began a study to observe the progress and outcome of untreated syphilis in black men, but over the next forty years they lied to the men they recruited, by telling them they were being treated. At least twenty-eight of the participants died from final stage syphilis, which causes tremors, blindness, tumours and organ failure. In 2010, Rebecca Skloot published a book called *The Immortal Life of Henrietta Lacks*. This told the story of how this 31-year-old black cervical cancer victim had cells harvested without her knowledge in the 1950s. Henrietta died, but her cells live on today. They have been used in countless medical developments – including vaccines like polio – and her family didn't even know, let alone share in the profits. It is no wonder that almost half of black Americans surveyed said they did not trust the Covid-19 vaccine enough to have it.

Although the pathway of race relations in the UK has been different in many respects, there is still a lot of vaccine hesitancy among ethnic minority groups in Britain. The Centre for Countering Digital Hate believes around 5.4million people living in the UK are so-called 'anti-vaxxers'. An article in the *British Medical Journal* in February 2021 noted one study that highlighted black, Pakistani and Bangladeshi people are more likely to be vaccine hesitant, and younger people aged 18–25. Even non-white medical workers are statistically less likely to have the vaccine. Black Caribbean and African populations have a 20 per cent less uptake of other vaccines as well, such as flu, compared to their white counterparts.

While it is easy to blame misinformation, ignorance or prejudice for an anti- or ambivalent vaccination stance, the BMJ article is clear: it is a failure of public messaging. The report says, 'Trust is eroded by systemic racism and discrimination, previous unethical healthcare research in black populations, under-representation of minorities in health research and vaccine trials, and negative experiences within a culturally insensitive healthcare system.'[10]

The NHS was established to offer healthcare equity, but healthcare equity can only truly be delivered along with social equity. Science alone cannot win over the hearts and minds of people who have a history of being let down by the very people paying the scientists. Truly accessible healthcare isn't just free at the point of use – it is provided without judgement, prejudice or discrimination, and it works for the people who need it, rather than pushing up against them.

Part III

Post-Welfare State Britain; Modern Disease and the Public Healthcare System

Chapter IX

The Big, Fat, Epidemic – How Obesity Shapes Public Health Care

'Do you know what the number one health risk in America is? Obesity. They say we're in the middle of an obesity epidemic. An epidemic like it is polio. Like we'll be telling our grand kids about it one day.
The Great Obesity Epidemic of 2004.
"How'd you get through it, Grandpa?"
"Oh, it was horrible Johnny, there was cheesecake and pork chops everywhere."'

> – Comedian Greg Giraldo from the song,
> *Underwear Goes Inside The Pants* by Lazyboy, 2004

I t's impossible to write a book that looks at epidemics throughout history without mentioning obesity. Disease and the burden it places on public healthcare have changed remarkably in the last 100 years, and today the maladies that affect OECD countries are more lifestyle related than anything else.

According to the study *The Global Burden of Disease*, published in *The Lancet*, 4.7 million deaths globally were linked to obesity in 2017 – that's four times more people than died in road accidents, and five times more than died from HIV/AIDs. It is a risk factor for the world's leading causes of death, including heart disease, stroke, diabetes and cancer.

This is a marked change from a century ago. According to the Office of National Statistics, in the UK in 1915 the most common cause of death was tuberculosis. But by 1955, just forty years later, it was heart disease. By 2015 the most common cause of death was almost evenly split between heart disease and obesity-related cancers such as rectal and colon. Tuberculosis is an infectious disease – and other diseases that commonly killed people around 1900 included flu and gastrointestinal bugs; all communicable diseases. These illnesses are, from a public health perspective, related to sanitation and the standard of medical care available. While it is possible to be born with diabetes, and have a genetic risk for certain cancers, these non-communicable diseases we suffer from today at epidemic levels are more often than not caused by our lifestyle.

Our way of life, in places like Europe and America at least, has changed to a point where the world now would not be recognisable to someone from a century ago – and that includes the maladies that affect us. The way we live is directly responsible for obesity, which is a risk factor for the biggest modern medical killers of humankind. Obesity isn't a new thing. The risk of disease related to body size was recognised by Hippocrates in ancient Greece. Every British school student knows how fat Henry VIII was, and historians now believed he suffered from diabetes brought on by consuming around 5,000 calories a day. His death at 55 was attributed to natural causes, but was no doubt hastened by obesity – he gained around 50kg after a jousting injury at the age of 44, and had poor circulation and permanently ulcerated legs for the last decade of his life.

However, being overweight – and the health problems that come with it – were rare before the twentieth century, and were also related to wealth and luxury. Up until the height of the European renaissance in the sixteenth and seventeenth centuries, being physically large was a mark of prestige; a display of your achievements. The Middle Ages was a period of want, where poor harvests, war and disease resulted in a general population that was chronically underfed. European men were on average about 70kg and women about 50kg. Compare that to the UK now, the average weight for a man is about 85kg and for women, 73kg. Although the renaissance period re-characterised larger people as gluttons and made big body shapes less desirable, it didn't change the demographic who were affected by weight gain. Until the mid-twentieth century, generally only the very wealthy were overweight or obese, because the type and volume of food and drink needed to achieve that sort of weight gain was well out of the reach of the average person.

Let's pause for a moment to talk about what the terms overweight and obese actually mean. In order to clarify who is at a healthy weight and who isn't, the World Health Organisation uses BMI, or the Body Mass Index. This is a population-wide average that quantifies an individual's BMI against everyone else over a period of time. To calculate your BMI you must take your weight in kilograms and divide it by your height in metres squared. If you are a European woman of average height – about 1.67m – and average weight – about 70kg – then your BMI will be 25, which is the top end of what the WHO considers to be healthy or 'normal'. BMIs over 25 put you in the overweight zone, while a BMI over 30 puts you in the obese zone. In the UK, there are three categories of obesity. Class 2 obesity is the next level up, with a BMI over 35, and class 3 obesity is a high-risk group for health concerns with a BMI over 40.

There has been a lot of criticism of the body mass index calculations over recent years. The formula for calculating BMI is nearly 200 years old, having been invented in 1832 by Belgian mathematician Adolphe Quetelet. While it is a good indicator of a person's physical size, it does not accurately demonstrate body fat. My husband, for example, is very tall and very athletic. His BMI calculation places him in the overweight category but every medical professional he has ever dealt with has told him to ignore that. You only have to glance at him momentarily to see he is not overweight.

Muscle weighs more than fat and so, along with other variables such as bone density, negatively affects the BMI result. It therefore doesn't give a clear indication of the risk of health problems like high cholesterol. A high-performance athlete could have the same BMI as someone who is overweight, or at the lower end of the obese range, and yet they would not have the same health risks because of lifestyle factors left unconsidered.

There are cultural and genetic factors also left unconsidered. For example, Asian people are less likely to be obese according to BMI charts, but are at a greater risk of developing type 2 diabetes and heart disease at lower weights. In China, a recent study published in *The Lancet*[1] showed the prevalence of obesity at around 25 per cent for adults. Meanwhile, a study published in the *British Medical Journal*[2] showed the prevalence of diabetes in China at 11.2 per cent. In the UK, around 28 per cent of people are considered obese but the rate of diabetes is just 6 per cent. It is important to bear these issues in mind when thinking about BMI as a measure of health.

While the WHO are quick to say that BMI should not be used as a stand-alone reliable health indicator for individual people, when looking at population-wide statistics, BMI can be a very good indicator of the health of a country or region. At the moment, it is the only universal yard stick we have when considering obesity. In addition, when looking at the higher end of the obesity scale, BMI is a good indicator of body shape and health risk because it is very unlikely someone will achieve a BMI of 40 or above through athletics.

Looking at the way average BMIs have shifted over the last 100 years paints a worrying picture of our health as a species. Globally, 39 per cent of adults are overweight and 13 per cent are obese. In the UK, 36 per cent of adults are overweight and 28 per cent of adults are obese. In the USA, almost 43 per cent of adults are obese today, but at the turn of the nineteenth century only around 5 per cent of adults were obese. The frequency of weight gain has shot up since the 1950s, and the WHO say obesity globally has tripled since 1975.

While most Western people no longer worry about tuberculosis, a disease that used to kill millions but today is easily treated with antibiotics, it has been replaced with obesity and the diseases relating to it – which is arguably caused by the same thing that has allowed TB rates in places like the UK and the USA to decline: wealth.

In Victorian times, poor people living in rural areas had the healthiest diet. They ate lots of locally grown fruits and vegetables, and supplemented their diet with some whole grains and a little freshly caught fish. Meat was almost non-existent, and dairy was relatively limited. Today, very few people in the Western world eat like this. The relative increase in wealth of individuals compared to their historical counterparts, along with societal changes in the way food is produced and how we like to eat, have resulted in a world where weight gain is a normal side effect of life.

In his book, *Why We Eat (Too Much)*, London-based bariatric surgeon Dr Andrew Jenkinson likens the diet of Westerners to that of livestock being fattened up for market.

'I was sitting at a dusty roadside tea shop in rural India, when I noticed that the traffic had come to a complete standstill,' he says. 'In the middle of the road I saw the source of the traffic jam, a cow, sacred and revered by Hindus.'

He notes that the animal looked 'bedraggled', and although it was no doubt well fed and cared for by its devoted owners, 'It seemed slim and wiry compared to the cattle that I was used to seeing in the drizzly fields of England.' Jenkinson asked himself why well fed Indian cows would remain slim while British farm beef bulked up relatively easy. He found there were two key components to the answer that both apply to humans and the changes to our diet in the last century.

The first is about the food the cows eat. When farming started, 10,000 years ago in The Levant, the animals farmed ate natural foods like grass. This is what cows in India still eat. But today we feed our farmed cows a mix of grains and vegetable oils – unnatural foods for cattle that fatten them up quickly. In addition, the cows live in a confined space, not moving around much – whereas 'wild' cattle would roam for miles and miles, and early farmers used to drive their cows and sheep around the countryside to access the best and safest pasture.

Does strategy one for fattening cows feel uncomfortably familiar? I don't know what your day has been like, but for many people it will have involved sitting mostly still at a desk, with sedentary periods punctuated only by a trip to the kitchen to get foods like toast and pasta salad. Jenkinson says; 'This type of change in diet, toward more grain and oil-based foods, when mimicked in the human population, causes a similar change in size – people will get bigger and fatter. On the whole, we are no different in our metabolic biology to those farm cows.'

Our ancestors, right up to the late 1940s and early 1950s when obesity statistics began to change rapidly, would have eaten more fresh vegetables and fruit, and would have been much more physically active than today. But the mechanisation of industry means less physical labour. A survey by Workplace Insight showed that 81 per cent of workers are sedentary for four to eight hours a day. These days, most jobs are office based, most kids are sat at desks in school all day and our food is mass-produced and heavily processed, relying on cheap oils and grains to be produced in bulk. And it is plentiful – but more on that later.

Keeping cattle still and feeding them high-fat, high-carb food is only half the picture. You see, we have been told by dieting gurus over the years that maintaining a healthy weight is all about energy-in equalling energy-out. So surely people just need to eat less and move more? Get off the bus one stop early, exchange a chocolate bar for some fruit … But Jenkinson says it is not that simple. In fact, many of the people he sees at his NHS surgery in London – clinically, chronically obese people – have tried very, very hard to lose weight, or even to just maintain their weight, but have found that the lbs keep piling on. The only thing that works for them is the drastic measure of irreversible surgery. This is because of the second strategy that farmers use to fatten up cows, and that is selective breeding.

'In every herd of cattle there are individual differences between animals,' says Jenkinson. 'If some of the species are taller or shorter, bigger or smaller, or faster or slower, the individuals at the extremes of the spectrum may be more likely to survive unexpected changes in the environment.'

For example, if there was a famine, then the fatter cows with more energy reserves might be more likely to survive, which means the next generation of cows would automatically be more prone to putting on weight. They have inherited that characteristic, and perhaps the cows less likely to gain weight have died out. Farmers use this knowledge to select cows that will give more yield of beef at market for breeding programmes. They are deliberately increasing the average size of cows from generation to generation using selective breeding, in order to increase their profits.

Humans have also accidentally been doing this for hundreds, if not thousands, of years. In fact, this natural selection process, where a certain group of humans with certain characteristics survives to reproduce, has been occurring for our entire existence. It has in the past been referred to as survival of the fittest but in fact, it hasn't really got anything to do with being physically fit. It's about whether your genetic predisposition to certain factors meets the needs and demands placed on your body by the environment you are living in at that time.

In an earlier chapter, we talked about the development of farming. Until farming was a business, until the point of farming was to provide an excess of food to garner an excess of profit for the owner of the means of production, people regularly died of starvation. Through the Middle Ages in the UK, the population would swell to just over 6 million, only to be culled again by famine or disease – or both. The population of the UK only began to stabilise and grow after the fifteenth century, when farming became a more formalised business rather than just something people did to survive.

So, in the years before that, when a lack of food was a common cause of death, the people who died will have probably have been those who were not prone to storing fat. Already we see that selective breeding of humans, the genetics of those who survived because they had more energy reserves being passed on. But as society changed, food became more plentiful and more calorie dense, this tendency to store fat has actually worked against us.

Jenkinson turns to Samoa for a clear, modern illustration of this process. Pacific Islanders colonised the lands they now call home, like the islands of Samoa, by travelling from their place of origin by sea. They were excellent seafarers, at a time when many Europeans were still floundering in the shallows. They travelled thousands of miles in large, hand-carved boats, navigating by using the stars and the flight path of migrating birds. These ships were not for war – like today's space ships, they were for survival. They took everything with them they would need – food, clothes, medicine. Whole families travelled together from the very old to tiny babies. Men, women and children holed up together, for weeks, if not months on end, relying on each other, fish from the ocean and the supplies they had packed before they left. It was an incredible feat, but there would have been losses.

In *Why We Eat (Too Much)*, Jenkinson says: 'You can imagine the hardship and risk involved. Quite often only those people who were "strong enough" to withstand the starvation of a long trip survived to live in these islands. There was, therefore, automatically a huge selection bias for anyone settled there.'

Individuals with a predisposition to storing fat, or with slow metabolisms that could shut down when food was scarce, were more likely to survive the voyage – and therefore to pass their genes on to the next generation. Once settled, storms, famine and later disease brought by European sailors further reduced pool of genes being reproduced.

The Samoan population may be made up from people who are genetically more able to gain weight and store calorific reserves as this is what was necessary. But they were not, historically, an overweight population. Physical work, and a diet that comprised of fresh fish, fruit like papaya and a few vegetables like taro, meant that everyone maintained healthy weights. But after the Second World War, food imports began. High fat, mass-produced, grain and carb-heavy foods from places like America. By the year 2000, Samoa had one of the highest obesity rates in the world, at 93 per cent for adults.[3] This is a microcosm of what is happening globally as humanity as a whole move less, eat more – and more unnatural foods –

after having selectively bred ourselves for survival. This is what happens when a species that has evolved for one type of lifestyle suddenly finds itself living in a very different way.

The elephant in the room, however, is not the overeater themselves, but the type of food being eaten and the amount of it that is available. Since the end of the Second World War the focus of industry has been on making life easier. Fordism gave us the production line and as a concept it has been applied to pretty much every manufacturing process globally. This includes food. Farmers, and the food industry, know which crops are cheapest to grow, produce the highest yield, and how to process them in to a way which is edible and enjoyable. The result is many of the foods we enjoy today – cereal, bread, rice-bowls, instant noodles, microwave meals like lasagne and comfort foods like crisps and biscuits. They aren't just grain and oil heavy, but have also become packed-full of refined sugar as that has become cheaper too.

In OECD countries, the people who suffer from obesity are no longer the rich, but the poor. The cheapest foods on our supermarket shelves today are the 'canteen' foods Jenkinson refers to in his book. Foods made of the same ingredients used to fatten up cows for slaughter. Food is no longer a necessity, but a commodity, sold not on its nutritional value but on the taste, convenience level, price and value. People don't buy food they need, they buy the food that they like and can also afford. At one UK mainstream supermarket, the average cost of an apple is 50p, with a pack of six ranging from £2.40 to £2.80. Meanwhile, six chocolate and cereal bars cost as little as 61p. If you are a family of four on a low income then it will make more sense to your financial health to buy the snack bars even if the impact on your physical health is negative in the long run.

This is a truth that has been reflected in countless studies. A combination of cost factors, and a lack of understanding around what healthy food choices actually are (thanks in large part to misleading marketing campaigns by manufacturers) has resulted in a disproportionate number of lower income families finding themselves at the upper end of the scales – and at higher risk of obesity related disease. A 2017 study published in *Science Direct*[4] looked at socioeconomic inequality in the morbidly obese community. It found that in the UK there was a direct correlation between low-income families and people with lower levels of educational qualifications and morbid obesity. Another study published in the *British Medical Journal* in 2017 looked at longitudinal data for BMI in the UK. They looked at cohorts born in 1946, 1958 and 1970 and found a clear link between socioeconomic disadvantage and higher BMI in childhood and adulthood.[5]

Other studies have shown similar results in the US and China but with one worrying change in dynamic – the more recent the study, the less close the link is between obesity and poverty. Lower income families and individuals are still more likely to have a higher BMI, but so are the next income bracket up. In fact, in the US now, all but the highest socioeconomic strata of society are suffering from inflated levels of obesity. This could be because of lifestyle factors such as the perceived need for convenience food due to long working hours, and it could also be because of the 'selective breeding' issue Jenkinson raised. The fact that women are more likely to suffer from high BMI than men indicates that a lack of leisure time is also a factor. A Forbes article from 2019 quoted a study from the *International Journal of Environmental Research and Public Health* that showed men in Europe exercise and have more leisure time than their female counterparts, spending approximately 70 hours a year more engaged in sport, relaxation and self-care. That's eighty minutes a week.

The rise in obesity in the UK has directly affected our welfare state and health service. Although the media presentation of overweight and obese people is jolly and comic, it is in fact a public health emergency which is placing a burden on services and changing the make-up of the NHS. Type 2 diabetes, as an example, costs the NHS around £11bn a year.

Services offered by the NHS that have had to increase capacity as a direct result of obesity increasing are wide and varied. They include the things you might expect, such as services to help treat high blood pressure, high cholesterol, liver disease and gallstones. But other services with increased pressure in part at least because of obesity include things like infertility services, asthma clinics, mental health services and physiotherapy dealing with back pain and osteoarthritis. In fact, if you visit an NHS physiotherapist in the UK and you have a high BMI, as part of their treatment they will offer you voucher for a slimming club.

Within the NHS itself, measures have been taken to support staff who are time-poor and low paid to combat their own obesity issues. A financial incentive for hospitals to provide healthier food options in staff canteens was introduced in 2016, with all NHS trusts contractually obliged to deliver against hospital foods standards as of 2019.

Many commentators believe this fire-fighting approach to obesity is part of the problem, and are calling for a unified strategy to support healthier lifestyles before obesity becomes unmanageable. Within the NHS, this means an overhaul of medical education. It has been noted that during a five or six-year medical degree, a student might have one day of training relating to obesity at most. The low priority placed on understanding obesity among doctors has a knock-on effect of patients not being properly referred or understood when they seek help later on. The NHS are trying to tackle this in partnership with medical schools, by offering short courses and updated guidance.

In 2018, Dr Rangan Chatterjee told *The Food Programme* on BBC Radio 4 that 80 per cent of complaints he sees as a GP today are lifestyle driven – he says this is a considerable increase over the last thirty years. Chatterjee was one of a number of professional signatories on a letter to the General Medical Council, the Health Secretary and the Medical Schools Council in 2016 calling for all medical students to receive significant training in evidence based lifestyle interventions. But apparently, change is slow.

While the wheels of bureaucracy in the health service and medical training institutions struggle to turn, the cost of the obesity crisis to Britain continues to gain pace. In 2016, the UK government spent £5.2m on their 'Change4Life' healthy eating campaign. Weight loss surgery actually has a cost saving value in the long term, but it still costs the NHS £38m a year. Arguably the spend around obesity simply isn't enough. Junk food manufacturers spend around £140–£145 million a year on advertising; that's approximately twenty-seven times more than the government spends on healthy eating education.

The Obesity Health Alliance believe that this isn't a problem that can be managed by the NHS alone and that the government cannot outmatch private industry spend on advertising. They believe drastic, policy-based action needs to be taken restricting the ability to advertise unhealthy foods. In November 2020, Downing street unveiled plans to restrict junk food advertising and sponsorship that would result in some of the toughest digital advertising laws in the world. In March 2021, the city of Bristol banned ads for junk food, along with pay day loans and alcohol on council owned advertising hoardings. In 2018, London banned junk food ads on transport services like the iconic London Underground.

In a phone conversation with Dr Jenkinson in early 2021, he told me the response to Covid shows that massive change is possible.

> If we really understood weight regulation and the root causes of obesity, then doctors would lobby the government to say this condition is going to bust the NHS. Or certainly have a massive financial impact on the country. The government's responsibility is to look after the people. As we've seen with Covid, the government will go all out to protect population if they understand a condition.

Jenkinson says the focus of the British food scene should be cooking at home, connecting with family through food that is freshly prepared – and that tax on the sweet, processed foods that cause the health issues should be used to subsidise fruit and vegetables and pay for an education campaign. 'If people ate better then a lot of Western diseases like IBS and asthma would get better,' says Jenkinson. 'People need to know it's not about the calories in food, it's the actual type of food itself that does the damage. It is having a profound effect on the NHS.'

Without a change in mindset about the cause of obesity, and the understanding that it is a medical condition in its own right, and not something relating to a lack of will-power or the choices of the individual, our society is on track for future medical disaster. To avoid it, over the next decade, the NHS will have to completely transform its approach to treating and managing lifestyle based conditions in a way that will require cross-agency cooperation, legislative support and an overhaul of funding priority focus. It is likely that for our children and grandchildren, the health service and welfare state will look very different to today, shaped by the many maladies we have created for ourselves through modernisation.

Chapter X

HIV and AIDS – a Pandemic of Fear

'HIV does not make people more dangerous to know, so you can
shake their hands and give them a hug. Heaven knows, they need it.'

Princess Diana

In July 1982, a man named Terrence Higgins collapsed unexpectedly,
and was rushed to hospital where he later died, aged just 37 years old.
Higgins had been born in Wales but, realising he was gay at a young
age, had moved to London to be at the centre of the scene. He worked as
a Hansard reporter by day, and as a DJ at the iconic gay nightclub Heaven
in the evenings – which was where he collapsed. He was friendly, popular,
and a bit of a mentor to the younger gay men still finding their feet.
Although the hospital initially said the cause of death was pneumonia it
was unusually sudden. Later examination revealed Higgins had Acquired
Immunodeficiency Syndrome – AIDS, although at the time it was known
as GRID – Gay Related Immune Deficiency.

Higgins did not know he had AIDS, and he was one of the first
officially confirmed deaths from an AIDS-related disease, with the
first UK death recorded just six months earlier. It had only been in 1981
that San Francisco resident Ken Horne was retrospectively identified as
'patient zero' in the AIDS epidemic cutting across America and fanning
out through Europe. He had been reported to the Centers for Disease
Control in the USA with Kaposi's Sarcoma the previous year, a type of
skin cancer now known to be common in HIV patients.

In actual fact, more recent studies have identified people who probably
died from illness relating to AIDS long before Horne gained notoriety.
There are two types of Human Immunodeficiency Virus or HIV, known
as HIV-1 and HIV-2. HIV-1 was first identified in 1984 and is split
into four subgroups, with HIV-1(M) identified as the pandemic strain.
Traces of HIV-1(M) have since been found in the remains of one man
from the Congo dating back to 1959. In 1969, a 16-year-old boy called

Robert Rayford from Missouri died from pneumonia in very unusual circumstances which have since been attributed to AIDS. In January 1976, the daughter of a Norwegian sailor died unexpectedly. Then the sailor died and a few months later his wife as well. It was later confirmed from blood samples the sailor had HIV. A 30-year-old woman passed away in Kinshasha in 1977 from diseases likely related to AIDS, and all three of her children also died from infections that could have been AIDS-related.

Although people diagnosed with GRID, and later the more accurately named AIDS in the early 1980s were routinely given between twelve and thirty-six months to live, most of them would have been living with the virus for several years, perhaps a decade, before the symptoms brought them to the attention of the medical profession. At the time though, the medical perception of this virus was that it appeared suddenly and inexplicably and people seemed to die quickly. And at first, it was unclear how it was spread. This led to what can only be described as a moral panic, focusing attention on the core groups that seemed to be affected – drug users, sex workers and gay men.

We now understand HIV to be a zoonotic disease that began affecting humans at the start of the twentieth century. A type of lentivirus, which are known for their long incubation period, HIV viruses are the result of multiple cross-species transmissions of simian immunodeficiency viruses[1] (SIVs). Although the AIDS pandemic is primarily driven by HIV-1, the discovery of HIV-2 in 1986 in Western Africa offered medical researchers some clarity over the origins of the disease.

The two HIVs are distinctly different from each other, with HIV-2 having more in common with the simian virus. Many different strains of SIVs have since been discovered in Sub-Saharan species like chimpanzees, African green monkeys, and mandrills among others. These SIVs are mostly benign to their hosts who seem to have adapted to live with their presence. They are ancient viruses – in some species, SIVs have existed for 30,000 years.[2] Asian primates do not naturally live with SIVs and when they contract an SIV, they end up with AIDS like humans.

SIVs are likely to have crossed into the human populations in West Africa via bush-meat hunting. Small, tribal communities could have been living with – and dying from – AIDS for decades before it came to the attention of the West in the late 1970s. Globalisation is credited with the spread of this virus into America, and on to Europe.

It has taken decades of dedicated research to understand this complex virus, but forty years ago, around the time Terrence Higgins died, there was a lot of confusion, misinformation and fear. This affected how the NHS dealt with both the disease, and patients of the disease. One man, a haemophiliac who contracted HIV through a blood transfusion in the UK as a teen, recalled how he was given the diagnosis in 1985.[3] He was just 16 years old, and was given three years to live. The nurses at the clinic told him he must never have sex.

When the five-part Channel 4 drama *It's a Sin*, which follows the lives of a group of gay men in London in the 1980s, was released in the UK in January 2021, many NHS workers took to Twitter to share their memories of those early years of treating AIDS patients in British hospitals. Some of the stories are truly heart-breaking. Staff too afraid to enter a dying patients room to bring them food. Doctors and nurses wearing unnecessarily high levels of PPE to attend to a patient. AIDS had become the new leprosy of the twentieth century.

This treatment wasn't universal though. One nurse, Sue Carrington from Bristol, shared in the media how well informed and compassionate staff were in the haematology unit where she worked. She said when she had to cover shifts on general wards and in surgery, sometimes things got 'silly'. But the poor bedside manner some patients experienced was driven largely by fear of catching the disease rather than judgement over a patient's lifestyle. In America, it was reported some hospitals were refusing to treat patients who were in the so-called high risk group for HIV, but here, in the UK, that was never an option. NHS staff simply got on with the job.

By the end of 1984, forty-six people had died from AIDS-related illness and there were 104 AIDS cases. Terry Higgins' partner Rupert Whitaker was one of those cases. Diagnosed with AIDS after Higgins' death he was given just twelve months to live. Today he is one of the longest living people with AIDS and is a psychiatrist specialising in the effect of HIV, and a qualified immunologist. In 1984, with a group of Higgins' friends, Whitaker set up the Terrence Higgins Trust to try to educate about AIDS and support those directly affected. Terry's experience, his own experience, and that of friends who were diagnosed was the driving factor. What they wanted to do was offer a human-rights based response to this medical problem. They changed the conversation and that turned out to be essential in effectively battling the pandemic.

The Terrence Higgins Trust had been involved in health education since before they were even a registered charity. In 1985, they were invited to their first meeting with the government. The Health and Social Security secretary Norman Fowler, now Lord Fowler, and Sir Donald Acheson, the chief medical officer, realised the government had not acted quickly enough. Needle exchanges were set up, and the newly developed test became readily available on the NHS. The Department of Health published advice on AIDS aimed at medical staff in the NHS. But more needed to be done to fight misconceptions about who was at risk. A bold advertising campaign was conceived, one that would shock the public in to paying attention and cut through the talk about who was at risk. The Terrence Higgins Trust consulted on the campaign, which was produced by agency TBWA and released in 1987.

I don't think anyone born before 1983 could forget the monolithic tombstone, or the ominous, Titanic-sinking iceberg and those chilling words – AIDS: Don't Die of Ignorance. Billboards, magazines and newspapers, and our nightly TV screens broadcast these adverts that offered clear messaging – everyone was at risk, and everyone needed to take action to protect themselves and others. As public health campaigns go, it has been described as one of the most effective of all time, despite some criticism for its over simplified message. One 1993 analysis noted a 46 per cent increase in HIV testing rates after the TV campaign.[4] Another study noted that the greatest increase in demographic getting tested was among heterosexuals with no other risk factors (such as intravenous drug use) – a group who may have previously (wrongly) seen HIV as not their problem.[5]

The first dedicated HIV ward was opened at Middlesex Hospital in 1987 by Princess Diana, who forever changed the public view of transmission risk by shaking a hand with an AIDS patient. Anecdotally, many remember this as a watershed moment after which patients experienced real change in terms of compassion. In his book, *Epidemics: Hate and Compassion from the Plague of Athens to AIDS*, author Samuel K. Cohn Jr notes how compassion-fuelled volunteerism to help those with HIV and AIDS – always present within certain communities – had become quite mainstream in America and Europe by the mid-'90s. As we have previously seen, pandemics flourish in a society full of stigma. By breaking down those barriers, the medical problem of HIV and AIDS could be more effectively addressed.

Perhaps one of the most beneficial aspects of the NHS in the AIDS pandemic has been the availability of free testing and healthcare, and free or discounted medication. When AZT, the first drug certified in the treatment of HIV, became available on prescription in the UK in March 1987, the uptake was huge. Meanwhile in the USA, the cost of medication was often a barrier. With a price tag of around $8,000 per year, that's more than $18,000 in 2021, treatment was not available to everyone. Even if you could afford health insurance, some insurers did not cover the cost of prescriptions. And if you became too unwell to work, then your health insurance might disappear along with your career. This is still essentially the case today. While the UK government set up a Cabinet Committee to address the AIDS crisis in 1986, it wasn't until 2010 that the US launched a National HIV/AIDS Strategy under President Obama's leadership. In Great Britain, the relationship between healthcare, welfare and politics was firmly established in 1948 but in the USA, healthcare is still viewed very much as the realm of the private individual.

There are now over forty Anti-Retroviral Treatment (ART) medications available to treat HIV, and in the UK, you can see a specialist doctor at a specialist clinic without a referral from your GP. You can have your medication delivered, or get it from a specialist pharmacy – your local pharmacy does not need to be involved. These are measures that have helped reduce the stigma and increase the privacy of HIV patients. HIV medication is free, and patients will also be offered counselling – something not always readily available in other countries with different medical systems. In the UK, 98 per cent of diagnosed adults are on ART and while this isn't a cure, the goal is to reduce viral load to the point where it is undetectable, and then the virus cannot be passed on.

Currently, 97 per cent of HIV positive people in the UK are virally suppressed according to Avert.org. One 2018 study, published in the *Journal of Public Health*, noted that many patients who were tested and/or received their diagnosis outside of the UK felt their experience had been 'worse than necessary'.[6] The same study also noted that with such a variety of people affected; straight, gay, drug users, sex workers, people infected by medical products, people born with HIV and people who became HIV positive through work, a variety of approaches to diagnosis and programmes of follow up care are necessary – and the NHS doesn't always meet the mark on that front.

Ongoing research into improving social and palliative care of HIV patients is happening in most NHS trusts to improve this situation. Many NHS trusts are also actively involved in research into drug therapies. Professor Jonathan Weber, Dean of the Faculty of Medicine at Imperial College London since 1991, got involved in AIDS research back in 1982. His mentor, Professor Philip Marsden, had returned from a trip to New York talking about a new disease that appeared to be affecting a lot of gay men. He wanted to look for this disease in London. Weber, then a young doctor at St Mary's Hospital with an interest in diseases that could be sexually transmitted, got involved with this project readily. He began studying the immune systems of gay men and discovered that many of his cohort of 400 had a low number of CD4+ T-cells, as well as swollen lymph nodes indicating they were trying to fight an infection. There was no blood test for HIV or AIDS at the time, but Weber felt confident these men were infected. He said later that it was a 'chilling insight' into the scale of this new epidemic.

Weber said since the first AIDS patient was admitted to St Mary's in 1982, they have always had an in-patient with the virus. By 1985 they had two full wards of mostly men with HIV and their work focused around fighting the opportunistic infections that take advantage of the poor immune system. By the late 1980s they were experiencing one death a day on the wards at St Mary's alone. But new drugs were starting to be developed and Weber set up an early clinical trial in 1991 that discovered, in 1994, that by combining ART drugs together you could prevent HIV from developing into full blown AIDS. This research was a game-changer for patients, and is the platform for the HAART combination therapy treatment of HIV today. Weber was also a founding editor of the journal AIDS in 1987, which has helped share international research and collaborations. He is currently overseeing the first ever European HIV vaccine efficacy trial in Africa, using an experimental vaccine developed at Imperial College.

NHS work on AIDS has extended out to other affected communities around the globe. According to the UN, of the 34 million HIV positive people worldwide, 69 per cent lived in Sub-Saharan Africa as of 2015. In 2013, the NHS started a two-year communication campaign in Africa, funded by the Department of Health, supporting positive messages about HIV testing and condom use. The NHS is also involved in a number of

UK-based projects, targeting Black African communities who may be at greater risk of HIV. For example, the Forth Valley African Health project is delivered in partnership with NHS Forth Valley and Waverley Care – Scotland's HIV and Hepatitis charity, while BHA, a health equality charity, work with a number of NHS bodies in England to provide better access to education, testing and care for African people living locally.

British research isn't just focused on medical needs, but also supporting end of life care, education for those with HIV, and reducing stigma. The two-phase PARTNER study, which demonstrated that if you had undetectable levels of HIV in your bloodstream, then you could not pass the infection on through sex. The study was led by Professor Alison Rodger from University College London and it was funded by the National Health Institute of Research. As well as helping to reduce the general stigma of HIV, the result also boosted testing and adherence to combination therapy among HIV positive people. Rigshospitalet in Denmark, the University of Amsterdam and CHIP – Centre of Excellence for Health, Immunity and Infections in Copenhagen were also involved.

A collaboration between the National Institute for Health Research (NIHR) and six British universities has seen a group of clinical researchers working on a cure since 2010. Called CHERUB – Collaborative HIV Eradication Reservoirs: UK BRC – their work focuses on how to eradicate the HIV virus that lives inside CD4 cells (also called T-cells) in a patient's body, called the reservoir. HIV positive people with no viral load who stop taking their ART would find the virus quickly re-established itself in their body. The only way to cure them completely would be to wipe these reservoirs out. Although a long way off, they believe a cure is very possible.

On 22 July 2019, Health Secretary Matt Hancock launched the Independent HIV Commission and pledged to end new HIV transmissions by 2030. Supported by various charities like the Terrence Higgins Trust, the commission undertook the task of figuring out how to meet this target. Their final report, published on 1 December 2020 – World Aids Day – is a roadmap to England becoming the first country to end HIV transmission for good.

Despite this great track record and lofty ambitions, the NHS still doesn't always get it right. When Pre-Exposure Prophylaxis, or PrEP, became available, initially NHS England refused to fund it. The decision, made in June 2016, came after a long period of deliberation during which many other countries, including the USA and Kenya, allowed it on to the market. This new type of HIV drug is taken before sex to prevent infection, and was considered the most effective way to prevent new infection beyond sexual abstinence. It also, for the first time, put the control firmly in to the hands of the HIV negative individual. It meant that they didn't have to second guess their partner's disclosure, or fall victim to a split condom. With 1 in 16 British people with HIV unaware of their own infection, it also reduced the chance of accidental spread. Ultimately, it would save the NHS billions of pounds, as it is much cheaper to prevent an infection than to treat it.

NHS England said they felt it was an issue for local authorities to deal with, potentially making access to PrEP a postcode lottery. Although pressure groups, including the Terrence Higgins Trust, had that decision overturned in court, NHS England's response was to announce a three-year trial with the numbers capped at 10,000 people. This sat at odds with the British government's commitment to eradicate HIV by 2030. An uncapped study began in Wales in 2017 and, at the time of writing, there had been no new HIV infections since it started. Scotland made the drug available in April 2017, a fully funded permanent roll out with no trial. An uncapped pilot of the drug is also running in Northern Ireland. It wasn't until October 2020 that it was announced PrEP availability would be uncapped in England. Many involved in the campaign felt these decisions were ripe with homophobia. There are currently just over 100,000 people living with HIV in the UK, a prevalence of 0.17 per cent. Infection rates have been dropping steadily

When AIDS first hit, it seemed like a once in a lifetime epidemic, the likes of which we'd never see again. But as the calendar rolled over into the twenty-first century, we began to understand how this had only been the beginning. The age of pandemics was truly upon us.

Chapter XI

From SARS to Covid, Pandemics in the Twenty-first Century

'Pandemics do not occur randomly. From malaria and influenza to AIDS and SARS, the lethal microbes have come, in the first instance, from animals, especially wild animals. And we increasingly know which parts of the world pose the greatest risk for future incursions.'

Nathan Wolfe, Ph.D

In November 2002, a farmer was admitted to hospital in the Guangdong province of China with an unidentified respiratory disease. He died shortly after, and no one knew why. Over the following week, a number of other people were admitted to hospital with similar symptoms. In Canada, the Global Public Health Intelligence Network (GPHIN) picked up a number of newspaper articles from China, talking about a flu outbreak. Part of GOARN, the Global Outbreak Alert and Response Network for the World Health Organisation, they reported these findings in early January 2003. Just a week later a patient was admitted to Sun Yat Sen Memorial Hospital in Guangzhou who was later identified as a super spreader.

About one in every five people globally are super spreaders, meaning that they transmit viral infections more readily than most, although we don't yet know why. Within weeks the infection had spread across the region. On 11 March 2003, it reached Hong Kong. On 12 March, the WHO issued a global alert for this new disease, SARS-CoV-1.

SARS, which stands for Severe Acute Respiratory Syndrome is a coronavirus, and until recently it was not clear where it came from. In 2017, Chinese researchers announced they had been able to trace the infection to horseshoe bats in Yunnan. Like HIV, SARS is a zoonotic virus that has passed through one or more species before reaching humans. Unlike

HIV, SARS was airborne and so easier to catch. It had a short incubation period and a mortality rate of about 10 per cent. It was perfect pandemic material, and suddenly all eyes were on China and Hong Kong.

The patient who took SARS from China to Hong Kong infected sixteen other people, who travelled to Canada, Singapore, Vietnam and Taiwan. When an American businessman died in Vietnam on his way home from China, the North American and European media started paying attention. This disease looked like a real threat. In the UK, the Health Protection Agency – a precursor to Public Health England – ramped up efforts to deal with the potential threat.

SARS has been described as the first major emerging infectious disease of the twenty-first century. It tested many aspects of public health systems, locally and internationally, in a new digital age. Although, in the end the UK only ever had four cases, SARS became the yard stick by which the country could test and modify its multi-pronged response. Among the issues that needed to be addressed were the legal base for public health action should it have been needed, systems in place for exit screening overseas travellers, and the capacity of existing systems – particularly health care – should cases have surged. The way we responded to SARS was considered a baseline framework for how to handle future pandemic threats.[1]

In a 2006 paper entitled Lessons Learned from SARS,[2] the authors talk about how the necessary global response to the pandemic laid the foundations of international collaboration. Coordinated by the WHO, field teams were sent to SARS hot spots to help manage the outbreak, and the UK's involvement facilitated ongoing information sharing – an essential element of containing pandemics in this day and age. This proved crucial when, on 15 March 2003, word was sent that a flight was en route to Germany with a potential SARS patient on board. Authorities would have to move fast to intercept the flight and isolate the patient, as well as test everyone else on board. The UK realised that should this happen here, it would require a coordinated response team.

Under Tony Blair's Labour government of the time, a taskforce was formed, including the NHS, health departments, national surveillance centres and representatives from Scotland, Wales and Northern Ireland. Their role was to provide surveillance, a management strategy for containing outbreaks and public health messaging and they were advised by a specialist team. A digital database to track cases and outbreaks was also designed, as existing software would not have coped with increased data from an outbreak. Although never fully used at the time, these systems and structures became the cornerstone that would inform future pandemic response.

The last case of SARS was in 2004 and the disease is now considered to be eradicated in humans. Although we developed neither a cure or a vaccine, cross-border cooperation and the containment of those who were infected resulted in the virus simply blowing itself out. There were just over 8,000 cases worldwide, and just under 900 deaths. Despite the fact the full pandemic potential of SARS was never realised, the risk captured the public imagination. This virus had shown for the first time outside of Hollywood the real potential of a virulent communicable disease to travel across borders at lightning speed.

In 2009, the UK got the chance to test some of the systems put in place during the SARS outbreak. But the next disease to threaten the globe wasn't a novel virus never seen by humans before, it was H1N1 – the influenza responsible for the Spanish flu. In 2009, it became known as the Swine flu pandemic.

In a period of just a few years in the early twentieth century, H1N1, then considered an avian flu, wiped out around 100 million people worldwide. But antigenic drift, the process by which flu viruses adjust themselves, transformed it from a super killer into just another a seasonal variation. But by mid-2008 the H1N1 strain had travelled through birds, humans and pigs extensively, rearranging itself into something a bit more worrying that seasonal flu.

The pandemic started on a pig farm in central Mexico, with the first human case identified in 2009, and it began to spread quickly among travellers. Once again, the WHO announced their concerns over its pandemic potential, officially naming the virus A/H1N1pdm09. Young people were especially vulnerable to catching it because of their lower immunity due to a lack of exposure to H1N1, and they were also more likely to experience complications including some unusual neurological problems. By June 2009 the WHO declared it a pandemic. By July 2009, there were 110,000 confirmed cases in the UK. A second wave in Autumn rose to a further 84,000 cases.

After their dry run in 2003, the Health Protection Agency and the NHS felt better prepared for this potential pandemic. The first confirmed case in the UK was on 27 April. Just a few days later, on 30 April, a public health campaign was launched with the slogan, 'catch it, bin it, kill it'. As soon as cases were detected among children in the UK, local schools were closed and advice was issued about isolating cases in workplaces. The approach was regional, pragmatic and evidence based.

Contact tracing was launched for passengers entering the country from high risk areas, although this was abandoned just a few months later in favour of a treatment option. The drug Tamiflu was made available to anyone reporting symptoms, with the government confirming it had a stockpile of the drug. The National Pandemic Flu Service was launched, an online and telephone based system that allowed the public to quickly ascertain if their symptoms were flu related without having to come into contact with a doctor. By October a vaccine had been developed and was being rolled out at a good pace, but the pay-off was no seasonal flu vaccine could be developed and administered that year. There simply weren't enough resources.

Swine flu cases began to decline sharply after the UK winter, and by late 2010 it had become a seasonal variant once again. Although there were only 18,499 confirmed deaths globally, it is estimated that around 280,000 people actually died from Swine flu. There were 457 deaths in the UK. Studies have shown as many as 1.4 billion people could have been infected.[3] However, over all, the virus had at least 20 per cent fewer casualties than the WHO had predicted. This was later attributed to latent immunity to H1N1 in older people, who would have been more vulnerable to complications. Although it was felt the UK dealt with the outbreak well, it got many in government asking – would we have coped if it had been more serious?

There are two interesting discussions from the 2009 pandemic that have an ongoing resonance. One is the decision not to make face masks compulsory. At the time, it was felt that as face masks do little to protect people from catching a flu virus, there was little point in introducing them as a precautionary measure. In addition, it was felt that face masks might make people complacent and therefore less likely to follow more necessary precautions such as washing hands. As we shall see, the view on this would change dramatically just over a decade later.

Another side story of this pandemic is related to the clinical research behind Tamiflu. According to the *British Medical Journal*, the UK government had been stockpiling this drug for some time. When the pandemic hit, they commissioned a review of an existing report on the medication by the Cochrane Policy Institute. Early on in the review, the panel received concerns about the original clinical trials. Apparently, a key piece of evidence relating to the claim that Tamiflu reduced the risk of secondary complications had been based on a series of ten trials by the manufacturer themselves, eight of which were unpublished.

The panel repeatedly requested additional data relating to the claim, but as the months wore on that data was not forthcoming. It also became apparent that neither the WHO, the EMA in Europe or the CDC in the USA had seen or vetted this data. Tamiflu was rolled out during the pandemic and it wasn't until 2013 that the Cochrane review panel finally had access to all the relevant information. They then concluded that the claim Tamiflu reduced the possibility of secondary complications was false. Tamiflu does help relive flu symptoms and reduce the period of sickness by one or two days. In an investigation, the *BMJ* uncovered some conflicts of interest among the scientists recommending Tamiflu to the WHO, as some had previously worked for the manufacturer and this had not been disclosed. This has certainly shone a spotlight on clinical trials, their veracity, and the conduct of those involved in recommending medications, which again would become particularly important a decade on.

In November 2010, the new UK coalition government between the Conservatives and the Liberal Democrats published a paper called, 'Healthy Lives, Healthy People: Our strategy for public health in England'. It proposed a reorganising of the NHS under a new bill, the Health and Social Care Act, which was eventually passed in March 2012. It created a new executive umbrella body, answerable to the Secretary of State; Public Health England (PHE).

PHE started functioning in April 2013, taking on all the functions of the now defunct Health Protection Agency, along with those of seventy other organisations. Regional Strategic Health Authorities were abolished, and much of the work of observing and tracking public health, screening, diagnostics and advising on social policy relating to health now fell to PHE. Community health services and social care, like GUM clinics, substance misuse prevention and Child and Adult Mental Health Services, were returned to the local authorities. (This is where the confusion over the responsibility for PrEP discussed in the previous chapter seems to have originated – because NHS England saw it as a local sexual health issue, while AIDS campaigners felt that it was a national health issue as HIV is not solely transmitted by sex.) NHS England was created to oversee budget and planning. There was already an NHS Wales, an NHS Scotland and a Health and Social Care body in Northern Ireland.

Part of the role of the PHE was to support public education around chronic illnesses, many of which had lifestyle factors involved. They were also the overseers of research into threats to the health of the nation like cancer. PHE also held responsibility for tracking and monitoring outbreaks of contagious diseases, and for pandemic planning.

In the decade between Swine flu in 2009 and the emergence of Covid-19, several more zoonotic viruses have been cause for concern. But none of the main ones; MERS, Zika and Ebola, have had the feared pandemic impact, the benchmark of which was set by Spanish flu. Ebola is spread by contact with infected bodily fluids, which means health workers and the families of patients are most at risk. This has made containment effective so far, and the handful of British citizens who have contracted Ebola have done so while working with patients in Sub-Saharan Africa.

MERS is another coronavirus that probably originated in bats, and is now spread via camels. There have been almost 1,000 deaths globally since the disease came to our attention in 2012. However, human to human transmission is quite rare outside of hospitals. The greatest risk comes from direct contact with camels. The Zika outbreak of 2015–16 was geographically limited to parts of South America, and as Zika only causes mild symptoms in most people, wasn't of huge concern. Those at greatest risk were pregnant women as the virus can cause microcephaly, a severe skull and brain malformation in the developing baby. So, when news broke in early January 2020 of a mystery disease in China, you have to forgive many people for initially being quite sceptical.

Early reports of a virus running amok in Wuhan washed over much of the UK population, more concerned with the January sales than a mystery pneumonia thousands of miles away. The first death reported on 11 January 2020 was a 61-year-old man with multiple complications. Two weeks later and the virus had cropped up in Japan, Thailand, South Korea and even the USA, always among people with confirmed links to Wuhan. Public Health England casually moved the risk from 'very low' to 'low'. Meanwhile, Chinese authorities quarantined Wuhan and its population of 11 million – although 100,000 people had left before the deadline. It all still seemed very far away, even when the WHO declared a 'public health emergency of international concern' – the highest level of alert – at the end of January. Two patients had the virus in the UK, both were returning from overseas travel and both were quarantined and monitored successfully.

But in just a few weeks public opinion changed dramatically. On 28 February it was announced that the twentieth person to test positive for the virus (now called Covid-19, and related to that first SARS outbreak in 2002), in the UK had not been abroad recently. This was the start of domestic transmission. Covid was now on our doorstep. On the same day, a British man in hospital in Japan after contracting Covid on a cruise ship died. The first British citizen to pass away from the virus. Newspaper headlines over the next few days were apocalyptic in nature. 'Find the hidden virus carriers' begged the *Daily Mail*, while *The Express* boldly predicted, 'cities will shut down in virus battle plan'. Even the broadsheets weren't immune to panic. 'PM warns thousands will catch virus across Britain' said *The Independent* at the start of March. British people returning from abroad began to be tested, and suspected patients were placed in quarantine. Reports of food rationing, financial crisis and concerns the NHS did not have enough staff or resources were rife.

Over the next three weeks, life changed dramatically. People became increasingly more anxious about what the future held. Prime Minister Boris Johnson warned at the start of March that, in order to combat the virus which now stood at fifty-one cases across the UK, schools might have to close and gatherings be scaled down. A fifth of the workforce may be off sick, he said. On 11 March the WHO declared Covid-19 to be a pandemic. The next day the SAGE advisory committee showed the UK government new modelling data predicting half-a-million deaths. The government advised those who were vulnerable to stay home and shield, hand sanitiser and toilet roll sold out at supermarkets, and people began to bump elbows instead of hugging or shaking hands. Overseas, Spain, France and Italy went in to lockdown. In some places the military were called in for support. Outbreaks of Covid were recorded in schools among children who went skiing in Europe on their half term break.

By Monday 16 March, swathes of offices were closed and people were working from home. Supermarket shelves began to be cleared of tinned food, dried pasta and UHT milk and informal rationing at the checkout was brought in. By the end of that week the government had committed to a lockdown starting 23 March – all schools, colleges and business were to close and people were to stay home except for key workers like NHS personnel and supermarket staff. Non-essential shops, pubs, cafes, cinemas and bowling alleys would be shut. Many festivals in the UK announced they were cancelling. No one was to travel except in emergencies. In fact, you were not meant to leave home for any non-essential reason, except for once a day to exercise. It was unprecedented. Even in 1918 restrictions of this level were not brought in.

It is difficult to write about the human side of pandemics, even more so to write about one you have lived through. If you are reading this decades in the future, and you have no memory of the exceptional changes that bestowed British life in the space of just a few weeks, then believe me when I say – it was hard. I don't want to dwell on personal anecdotes here. There are so many stories already available. But sometimes I think back to the weekend before lockdown was announced and I am amazed by the things that we did. I'd travelled to London from Bristol on Thursday 5 March, and had been surprised to get a seat on the tube at rush hour. On the Saturday, my children and I took a train four stops into the North Somerset countryside, and rode our bikes to my parents' house. We had a roast dinner, stayed overnight and my dad gave us a lift home the next day. Little did I know that would be the last time I would see my parents for months – I didn't even give them a hug. On the Sunday afternoon, I popped to the supermarket – a trip that took me fifteen minutes. A week later, I queued in silence in a two-metre bubble for an hour-and-a-half just to get in.

The initial lockdown, scheduled for three weeks, went on in its absolute form for just under eight weeks in total, but restrictions were only lifted slightly at the end of May. Pubs and restaurants, for example, could not open again until 4 July and were only allowed to serve groups of six or less at outside tables. Although there was a constant, slow easing of lockdown restrictions over the summer months in 2020, including Chancellor Rishi Sunak's 'Eat Out to Help Out' scheme that attempted to kick start the hospitality sector with a government subsidy on food, restrictions were back in place by the end of October with a soft lockdown for a month, followed by another full lockdown including school closures from January 2021 through to mid-March. But the focus of public scrutiny during that first two-month period was on the way the government handled the pandemic, and the way the NHS handled the pandemic – with public opinion firmly polarised at each end of the spectrum.

In October 2016, PHE and NHS England had carried out a three-day pandemic simulation with healthcare professionals called 'Exercise Cygnus'. The purpose was to evaluate how well prepared the nation was for an outbreak of a pandemic virus. They modelled the outbreak on H2N2 influenza which had been responsible for the so-called 'Asian flu' outbreak in 1957 to 1958. In the UK, more than 9 million people were infected, with 14,000 deaths. H2N2 is now extinct in the wild. Around 950 people took part, including critical workers in the NHS, prisons, and government departments. The simulation was led by the Emergency Preparedness, Resilience and Response Partnership Group.

The simulation began at the theoretical seventh week of the pandemic with an estimated 400,000 deaths and more than 50 per cent of the population infected. Workers were told a vaccine was available but had not been rolled out. They had to come up with and execute a management plan under this high stress situation. There were fake news reports, a made up social media outlet and even mock COBRA meetings. The results of the simulation remained a secret for years. Later, one source who was involved said the report was simply deemed to terrifying to be made public. But eventually, in May 2020 at the height of the Covid-19 pandemic, it was leaked to *The Guardian*. Exercise Cygnus, it transpired, had resulted in a collapse of healthcare services, the country's systems too under-resourced and under-funded to cope with a disaster of pandemic proportions.

This revelation was not met with surprise, but rather with disgust by most of the public and media. Boris Johnson's government, which had only been elected months before on 19 December 2019 with 43 per cent of the vote, had now come under harsh criticism for perceived delay in taking action as Covid-19 emerged. Other countries such as New Zealand and Taiwan took early, decisive action while case numbers were still low, which appeared to have been lifesaving decisions for their populous. The message from 10 Downing Street was that we have to 'take the right steps at the right time', but when the UK finally went in to lockdown we already had a total of 335 recorded deaths and 6,650 positive cases.

When questioned on why lockdown didn't start earlier, the government repeatedly relied on the concept of behavioural fatigue – that if you started too early, people would get bored and break the rules. But an article in the *BMJ*[4] detailed how there was no scientific evidence for this claim. In fact, on 16 March 2020, 681 behavioural scientists wrote an open letter to government voicing their concerns on this issue. It appeared the government were not listening to their scientists. In June 2020, former scientific advisor to the government, Professor Neil Ferguson, said that introducing lockdown just a week earlier in the UK could have halved the death toll so far.

The emergence of the Cygnus report appeared to be yet further confirmation that the government had not paid attention when there was still time to make change. The Cygnus report listed four 'key learning' areas, alongside another twenty-two recommendations, which included further modelling to understand the capacity of the state care sector, research to ascertain how the public would respond to such a crisis, and the creation of a tactical plan to ensure smoother cross agency cooperation. Although Health Secretary Matt Hancock tried to reassure the public that everything recommended in the report was done, it soon became apparent this was not true.

On 25 October 2020, journalist Paul Nuki wrote an article in *The Telegraph* clearly demonstrating six key areas where progress had not been made, that directly affected the Covid-19 pandemic response. These included a recommendation to model patient surge capacity for NHS hospitals. He concluded this could not have been done because in March 2020, one reason for the slow decision around the next steps was that this type of data was still being collated.

Another issue exposed by Cygnus was 'silo planning' between regions and departments. There was no overview of pandemic response plans, or a united approach between the four nations and agencies with them. The report recommended a single body be set up to coordinate pandemic operations, but this was not done. Discrepancies between regions, nations – and even hospitals and clinics in the same area, has been a constant feature of the Covid-19 pandemic, causing confusion, anxiety and delayed testing. Another really shocking revelation was that schools were hit very hard in the Cygnus simulation, and it was recommended that a strategy was designed to pre-empt the need for mass school closures. Again, this was not done, and the government faced heavy criticism during the Covid-19 pandemic over the lack of clarity around the plans for schools, many of which were announced without consultation or warning.

Conversely, the NHS as a system, and the people who work within it, became the true heroes of the pandemic. The antithesis to Boris' bumbling bogeyman. This was demonstrated by the incredible grass roots phenomenon of 'Clap for the NHS'. Dutch national Annemarie Plas, who lives in London, heard about similar initiatives in Europe and advertised the idea on social media. She asked people in a message to stand on their doorstep at 8.00pm on Thursday 26 March and clap for a few minutes to show appreciation for key workers and medical staff risking their lives in the pandemic. It was picked up and promoted by national media and millions took part in the event, which was renamed 'Clap for Carers' in recognition of non-NHS key workers, and became a weekly feature of the pandemic until 28 May. It also inspired works of art, 'Thank You NHS' signs and rainbows placed in people's windows to show their appreciation for those on the front line.

Although not the original intention of Plas, the event was highly politically charged. In the early weeks of the pandemic the lack of Personal Protective Equipment in hospitals which placed staff at risk of infection was highlighted in the media. A shortage of scrubs, masks, eye protection, gloves and gowns were all highlighted by NHS staff angry at the hypocrisy of government ministers joining in the clapping. Many also took the opportunity to raise awareness of pay cuts, particularly among nurses, staff shortages and a lack of other types of essential equipment. Dr Meenal Viz, a pregnant consultant, began protesting outside Downing Street. Stories emerged of staff having to wear bin bags and home-made masks.

By mid-April more than fifty NHS workers had died after being infected with Covid. By January 2021 the number was thought to be around 850, with 52,000 NHS staff off sick. In an opinion piece posted in the *BMJ* blog section on 29 January 2021, Australian GP David Berger called for an end to the 'rhetoric of healthcare workers as heroes'. He described it as 'a damaging distraction from the legal and moral imperative to accord healthcare workers the same standards of occupational safety enjoyed by workers in other industries, such as construction or mining'.[5] An article in *Nursing Times* on January 2021 said that healthcare staff, although recognising the good intentions behind 'Clap for Carers', did not want to be clapped. They wanted fair wages, adequate resources, and for the public to adhere to medical and scientific guidelines.

In her book *Breath Taking*, published at the start of 2021, palliative care doctor Rachel Clarke described how the pandemic hit the NHS from her first-hand experience. She says:

> The Covid ward is humid and restive. We are on the move, no pausing or lingering, with strained expressions and a twitchy hypervigilance that is as exhausting and stifling as the masks we wear. It is all around us, the virus. It coats our clothes, our hair, the backs of our necks, the keyboards we type on, the surfaces we touch.

Clarke paints an expressive picture of her patients, many elderly, some with dementia, many at high risk from Covid, who could not have visitors and may not see their families again. She described the hospital like a ghost ship, rows of empty seats devoid of the sight and sounds she was used to – queues and flirting and swearing and lost visitors and confused patients. She is also animated in regard to her anger at the sacrifice made by many members of staff also at risk. Staff who disproportionately came from Black, Asian and other non-white groups. She talks of the distress felt by staff working at her hospital, the John Radcliffe Hospital in Oxford, when their own members of staff began to die. She doesn't sugar coat it – or her anger at the way the pandemic was handled. It is clear not just from Clarke's experience but that of many doctors and nurses that NHS frontline workers were placed at greater risk during the pandemic than is morally acceptable.

In the 2021 budget, a 1 per cent pay rise was announced for healthcare workers which many said was insulting. An independent review was called, and by July the government had increased the offer to 3 per cent. In real terms, this amounted to just an additional £1,000 a year for most nurses, and only about £500 a year for cleaners and porters – the overlooked essential workers who were at heightened risk during the pandemic. The Royal College of Nursing had demanded 12.5 per cent and said that 3 per cent was a pay cut in real terms, once adjusted for inflation. Not only did the government not improve their offer, the 2022 budget again saw a paltry 3 per cent pay rise offered after MPs had voted in a 2.7 per cent pay rise for themselves. The average salary of a nurse in the UK, it should be noted, is just over £33,000, while MPs receive just under £85,000 annually. The consumer price index in February 2022 showed consumer prices were on average 6.2 per cent higher than the previous year, and unions including Unison have warned a mass exodus of NHS staff is on the horizon.

The row over pay, set against the backdrop of the extreme risk NHS workers were exposed to during Covid, and the hypocrisy of the government clapping but not paying a fair wage, has come to epitomise the wider anger relating to years of underfunding of the NHS. After the Tory-leaning coalition government were elected in 2010, investment in the NHS rose by only 1.4 per cent each year, rather than the 3.7 per cent the service had enjoyed since its inception. While the government insisted it was still increasing funding, in real terms the NHS lost out on billions over the next seven years of 'austerity'. Sectors of the NHS that had been moved to Local Authorities under the 2012 reforms were hit even harder. An article in the British Medical Association journal from October 2020 called 'Austerity – Covid's Little Helper', puts the public health grant deficit at £700m over five years, as LA budgets were cut by one third. The row over funding and pay for NHS staff is as old as the NHS itself, but the Covid pandemic has certainly brought the urgency of the situation into sharp focus.

Sitting between accusations of government mismanagement and high regard for the NHS, is the incredibly successful vaccine story. The genetic sequencing for Covid-19, whose official name is SARS-CoV-2, was released by the WHO in early 2020. This allowed many pharmaceutical companies to get cracking on developing a potential vaccine. In fact, many companies had already started this work with other coronaviruses in mind, although a successful jab for this type of virus had not been produced before.

By March 2022, 50 million adults and teenagers had been fully vaccinated with two doses of the vaccine, and the vaccine programme has now been approved for children aged 5 to 11 years. An additional 38 million people have had a third or 'booster' dose. We are the forty-fifth most vaccinated country in the world with an uptake of 79 per cent of the population. The UAE is first, with 99 per cent vaccinated.

In February 2021, Health Secretary Matt Hancock admitted on LBC radio that his commitment to ordering enough vaccine for every adult early on was inspired by 2011 movie *Contagion*. In the movie, once a vaccine had been developed, society descends briefly in to chaos as no one knows how many doses are available or who should get them first. Hancock wished to avoid this potential. A clear order of age-based priority was also declared early on.

When it was announced a vaccine would become available just ten months after the initial development began, many people were sceptical. It usually takes years to develop vaccines and some sections of the public expressed concern that the testing phase had been rushed. Medical professionals and pharmaceutical agencies were quick to reassure the public. The British Society for Immunology went to great lengths to explain that the reasons vaccines usually take such a long time is because of delays in funding. The unprecedented financial support, opening up of resourcing, collaboration between professionals and availability of people happy to be part of clinical trials meant that the usual stages of the process could all be completed in a much shorter time period. Researchers already had a framework from SARS and MERS potential vaccine development to springboard the process. As we saw in relation to Tamiflu in 2009, the medical profession themselves are very good at self-regulation, and calling out processes where corners appear to have been cut, or claims can't fully be substantiated.

Another polarising government decision was the compulsory wearing of masks, introduced on 24 July 2020. There had been a lot of political resistance to this despite expert recommendation. Back in 2009, mask wearing was not seen as necessary by many facets of the medical profession, but during Covid that position changed. As the virus has a potential incubation period of two weeks or more, and as it became apparent that a high percentage of people could carry the virus and be asymptomatic (confirmed by South Korean researchers in late 2020) the British Medical Association pressed the government to make it a legal requirement. In a survey they conducted of British doctors, 86 per cent felt masks should be compulsory in situations where social distancing could be hard, like the supermarket.

Despite backing from the medical profession, the response from both businesses and public was mixed. Many supermarkets said they would not enforce the rule by turning shoppers without a mask away. Anti-mask protests broke out in some cities, including London, by groups who believed the state was encroaching upon their freedoms. Many of those protesters felt that the virus itself was a lie, part of a 'deep state' conspiracy. Others believed the virus was real but that it wasn't as much of a threat as had been made out and was being used to control the population. Most of the protests were calling for an end to lockdown restrictions as well.

Other members of the public took it upon themselves to police the use of masks. News outlets were rife with stories of people who had been verbally, or in some cases physically, abused for not having a mask on. Many of the victims were people with hidden disabilities exempt from wearing masks, and an education campaign encouraging understanding from the public was launched. Demand for the Sunflower Lanyard, which identifies someone with a hidden disability, increased dramatically as people sought an appropriate way of communicating that they had genuine reasons for not wearing a mask. Many businesses, such as HSBC and Sainsbury's, were quick to publicly support the scheme and explain what the lanyard meant to customers.

On 24 February 2022, the government officially ended all restrictions. They published the Living with Covid Plan, which called upon citizens to continue to act responsibly and offered advice on protecting the most vulnerable. There has been a lot of criticism from health and care workers about these restrictions being lifted. A significant easing of restrictions had begun in mid-2021, with the requirement to wear facemasks removed in July of that year, only to be reintroduced again in November after a surge in cases relating to a new variant. The Omicron variant, which was much easier to catch than previous Covid variants, swept across the UK forcing all four nations to back peddle on some of their Covid policy easing. Arguably, when restrictions were finally lifted in 2022, the pandemic was still far from over – and mask wearing and various social distancing measures are still common albeit voluntary. The pandemic and its effects are still so recent and raw, it is difficult to conclude this chapter with any sage observations about what came as a result. But as we begin to navigate through this post-pandemic period everyone is asking, what will happen next?

Chapter XII

Beyond the Welfare State – Where does Universal Healthcare go Next?

'Universal Basic Income is the only policy measure that will ensure protection for everyone, while giving the economy the fuel it needs.'
Fuad Alakbarov, activist

It is easy to look back through history and see the wars, the slavery, the famines and of course, the diseases, and reflect on how things have improved. However, one of the things that often escapes our attention, especially when looking at ancient history, is the natural egalitarianism that evolved alongside human society before capitalism became the default model for most of the world.

The hunter-gatherer societies of ancient times, which still make up 90 per cent of human historical existence, had a way of self-organising that ensured everyone's needs were met while no one individual was able to have more than their fair share. Sharing and cooperation were essential to survival.

In a 2005 paper on the topic, Frank Marlowe[1] noted that among forager societies, long, monogamous relationships were standard, with couples often choosing to live with either one of their sets of parents in a cooperative way. The grandparents could then provide care to children, and later, the children and grandchildren could care for elderly parents. The foraging model was one he calls central-place provisioners – the able went out to hunt and gather, leaving the less able in a secure location. Food was then brought back and shared between everyone. Ownership of property was almost non-existent, so conflict over possessions was rare. Everyone in the society had a role to play, with no amount of respect allocated to any one particular function over another. In many groups, hunting parties were made up of women and men.

Modern non-agricultural societies clearly demonstrate this set up. The Hazda people of Northern Tanzania are one of the last such tribes in

Africa. They own no livestock, and they don't grow or store food. They exist on a mostly plant-based diet of naturally occurring tubers and fruits with a little meat and honey. They move around the valley perched on the edge of the Serengeti, living in temporary shelters they make from grass and branches. They are, genetically speaking, one of the oldest human lineages and their lifestyle has largely remained the same since their oral records began tens of thousands of years ago. They are a living example of the first iteration of human society – flat hierarchy groups that took what they needed, living and supporting each other in a communal and respectful way.

Camilla Power, a senior lecturer in anthropology at the University of East London argues that egalitarianism was necessary for human evolutionary success. She says not only were human societies equal, but that this equality – or equity – was the baseline upon which we flourished. You can see this clearly in our biology, she says. Our eyes are called cooperative eyes – the dark iris on the white sclera means we can easily see what others are looking at, an evolutionary sign we worked in groups early on. A unique trait among primates, other species still compete with each other for resources in a way early man gave up on quickly. She also notes that other primates only stare into each other's eyes to threaten, where as we do this to acknowledge, connect and understand each other.

The menopause is another example of how we evolved to cooperate. Humans are the only land-mammal to go through menopause, freeing us up from the drudgery of constant pregnancy and birth other female mammals experience. Once we stopped having our own children, we could start caring for other children. This would in turn free up younger members of the community to fulfil other important community functions. Cooperative childcare is also limited among primates. While most Apes keep their children close by, humans have always had a strong tradition of babysitting. We trust each other enough to leave our children attended to by another person. Anthropologist Sarah Hardy argues this community childcare approach was essential in allowing our brains to expand to their incredible volume today – around three times bigger than the average chimpanzee. As babies are held by, look into the eyes of, and listen to the voices of, a variety of different people, their brains experience growth to accommodate all this new information and the emotional bonds that come with it.

So why did this egalitarianism come to an end? In an article in the *New Scientist* in 2012, Deborah Rogers argued that inequality is rooted in agriculture and the birth of surplus. Before we began farming, we only ever had what we needed, but as populations expanded and farming became professionalised and then industrialised, we invented the surplus. Since then, entire nation states have been constructed around the idea of a surplus – more food than we can eat, more natural materials than we can use, and more money than we can spend; often at the expense of others. Conflict and conquest have become second nature, with property ownership, materialism and excess the markers of individual success. Although inequality is not necessarily beneficial to modern society, it is not an evolutionary dead end we are stuck with. It's just that we've lost our groupthink.

In the last years of the eighteenth century, the Marquis de Condorcet, Nicolas, was in hiding. Having previously been heavily involved in the French Revolution, the mathematician and philosopher was now living under the threat of a death sentence after criticising the new constitution. To pass the time he wrote a book, *Esquisse d'un tableau historique des progrès de l'esprit humain* (Sketch for a Historical Picture of the Progress of the Human Mind), and in the last chapter he made an incredible suggestion. He suggested that, instead of leaving the welfare of the old, the widowed and the orphaned to the church and luck, that the state might want to help by giving them money. It was a simple problem of calculus, he said, and it made sense to fund people en masse in this way to avoid the misery of bankruptcy and corruption.

The first social insurance systems in Europe, launched in Germany by Bismarck in 1883, were based on Caritat's model. The underlying principle was not that some people needed assistance, but that all people were entitled to this support. This is also the basis of Nye Bevan's NHS. This idea of universal entitlement was a return to our egalitarian social principles, and quite a big step away from the means-tested 'benefits' model of most welfare states. It didn't judge the recipient's worthiness, because everyone was worthy of this help. But could this model of support be taken beyond healthcare, old age pensions and orphans? And what would the implications be?

English Radical Thomas Spence, who advocated for common land ownership long before Karl Marx put pen to paper, published a book in 1796 called *The Meridian Sun of Liberty*. In this booklet he argues that the wealth of a Parish, after all public expenditure has been covered, should be divided between each and every soul living in the Parish, young or old, male or female, working or not. What he is proposing is a Universal Basic Income – a minimum guaranteed level of personal income, granted to you by the state in honour of your existence, with no strings attached regardless of your station in life. This isn't a handout, or help, or philanthropy – it is what people are entitled to. Charles Fourier argued in 1836 that, as agriculture, industry and private land ownership had taken away the right of humans to forage and live in a way that meets all their needs, then the landowners should pay those people an equitable share of what has been taken to facilitate their subsistence. What he is saying is, in the absence of a traditional egalitarian society that shares natural resources, our new post-capitalist society should be sharing that one abundant resource we have created for ourselves but continues to be hoarded by the few – money.

Between the wars, in twentieth-century England, parliament hotly debated whether a UBI should be introduced. Labour Party member Dennis Milner argued forcefully for a 'state bonus' paid weekly to every household in Britain as a way to solve issues relating to poverty. Bertrand Russell, the highly lauded non-conformist political thinker, also advocated for a personal stipend to be paid by the state, 'sufficient for necessities'. Later, British Engineer Major Clifford Douglas proposed a system he called 'social credit', where each household would receive a regular dividend based on GDP. Economist George Cole agreed such a dividend would be beneficial not just in terms of fighting poverty, but to the economy as a whole, and Oxford economist James Meade argued this idea was central to both a just and efficient economy. He saw it as a solution to unemployment, as well as poverty.

However, these ideas remained just that, theoretical solutions pushed around the smoke-filled rooms of left-wing liberal intellectuals. They were never much more than after dinner conversation, although of course the model surely played some part in the conceptual formation of the NHS system and subsequent welfare state. In America in the 1970s, an attempt at policy was made. Nixon's Family Assistance Plan abolished the means-tested welfare programmes targeting poor families and instead offered a guaranteed income for workers with supplements. It was rejected by the Senate, however, and the Watergate scandal marked the end of further discussion.

Academically speaking, the idea of a UBI never really went away. In 1976, Dutch academic Jan Pieter Kupier recommended the separation of work and income as a health measure, having observed how sick some people made themselves either finding work, or in their job. In 1985, the Scientific Council for Government Policy recommended a 'Partial Basic Income' – a universal payment to help cover the basics. Around the same time in the UK the Basic Income Research Group was formed, which became the Citizens Income Trust in 1998. Similar groups were established in France and Germany. The Basic Income European Network was established in 1986. It is now the Basic Income Earth Network due to the global expansion of those interested in a UBI.

In 1982, Alaska became the first region in the world to implement a social dividend called the Alaska Permanent Fund. This modest, annual pay-out goes to every citizen resident in Alaska for more than six months, and is based on investments made off the back of oil industry profits in the 1970s. Because it relies on the stock market, it fluctuates each year, and it's more in line with what was proposed by the earliest thinkers – that profits made from the land would be distributed to the people of that land in some way – than an ongoing, reliable and unconditional basic income. However, research has shown that since the fund started there has been no decrease in full-time employment and an increase in part-time employment, waylaying some of the major objections raised by those who oppose a UBI.

The major opposition to a UBI has been from those who believe it is giving people something for nothing. Rather than seeing it as a redistribution of wealth along our natural, evolutionary, egalitarian lines, objectors believe it will fund crime, drug use, antisocial behaviours and result in higher unemployment as people no longer feel the need to work. The trialling of a UBI in a region is essential to determine whether these concerns are based on reality, or are simply a moral panic – a product of our often traditionally faith-based beliefs that hard work will solve all ills. If the Devil makes work for idle hands, what will people do if we pay them to be idle?

There have been several small trials across the globe. In India between 2011 and 2012, a short UBI trial was credited for increasing the education rate of young people by 25 per cent. The GiveDirectly scheme in East Africa makes unconditional cash transfers to families in poverty. In 2016, it launched a twelve-year basic income experiment in a region of Kenya that will give 6,000 people regular payments and monitor the impact. Perhaps the most impressive and promising study happened in Finland between 2017 and 2018.

During this two-year study, 2,000 unemployed people received a payment of 560 euros a month, no strings attached. The payments were not withdrawn or reduced if participants got a job. Crucially, participants didn't volunteer but were selected and were legally not allowed to opt out. This provided a great basis for trialling UBI across a demographic, rather than the results being skewed by volunteers already sympathetic to UBI. The outcomes for that group were compared against a control group of 173,000 people on unemployment benefits. The results were pretty impressive, with those receiving a UBI working more than the control group, and also reporting improved mental health, cognitive functioning and financial wellbeing.

In the UK, UBI Labs Sheffield launched, and secured backing from the Labour-led council in 2019 to support a UBI trial in the city. There are now thirty-five citizen-led UBI labs based in the UK, conducting small studies and engaging in political lobbying. A recent paper[2] noted the cost of a UBI in the UK would be £67 billion a year, or 3.4 per cent of GDP – that would pay every adult around £7,700 and every child £3,800 each year (with additional benefits still in place to support those with disability). It would eliminate absolute poverty, and reduce those living in poverty from 16 per cent to 4 per cent. But at the start of 2020 it was still largely a fringe movement.

The Covid-19 pandemic has changed many things, and one of them is the interest in UBI. Most middle-income families, it has been stated, are just one unexpected payment away from debt. A car breakdown, an emergency dental bill, a broken boiler – these are examples of some of the mundane things that could unbalance the financial equilibrium in even a moderately wealthy household. A December 2020 survey by finder.com showed the average British resident had less than £7,000 in savings and one in three has less than £600. Around 10 per cent had no savings at all. By March 2022, UK inflation was at a thirty-year-high with disposable income expected to fall by 2.2 per cent over the financial year creating the biggest recorded drop in living standards since 1956. The impact of the pandemic and the national shut down has brought the tenuous financial situation of the average Brit in to sharp focus.

In the middle of 2020, while British people were still trying to apply for a mortgage holiday and figure out the Self Employment Income Support Scheme grant, Spain introduced a basic income scheme for 850,000 of the nation's poorest families, offering them an unconditional pay-out of just over 1,000 euros a month. In Brazil, a similar scheme was introduced with a quarter of the population receiving a monthly payment of US $110 per month from March 2020. The result of that last scheme was poverty quickly falling to its lowest rate in forty years. It is the change in the political climate that has made these basic income payments possible – the pandemic has made people more open to the concept.

Supporters of a UBI argue the mental and physical health benefits, as well as the financial benefits, could be huge. A UBI could save the NHS money in the long run. An article in the *British Medical Journal* in January 2021 notes that poverty and 'stagnant income growth' are inextricably linked with poor health outcomes. They note one study that linked poverty with Covid-19 mortality, and that children in the lowest income bracket are 4.5 times more likely to develop serious mental health problems than their peers in the highest bracket.[3] The report goes on to say that evidence suggests reducing poverty is linked to better mental health and higher standards of nutrition, and that participants in UBI trials have reported better physical and mental health as a result. For a system that will cost less than Brexit, is less than the annual value of corporate tax breaks, and is less than 10 per cent of the total annual spend of the UK government, the gains seems to stack up.

Without urgent, drastic change to the way we implement the welfare state in the UK, the public healthcare system is untenable in the long term. According to the OECD's *Health at a Glance* report from 2016, the UK only has 2.7 hospital beds per 1,000 people, while Germany leads with 8.2 and even Serbia, one of the poorest nations in Europe, has 5.5. In 2017, the NHS had to launch a dedicated fraud agency to tackle £1.25bn a year loss in bogus prescriptions, fake supplier scams and internal price fixing. Missed appointments also have a high annual cost. But the biggest burden to the NHS since 2008 has been Conservative austerity-influenced budget cuts that have resulted in longer waiting times, a reduction in services and a lack of investment in staff, training and facilities.

According to a report by the WHO[4] in 2019, mortality rates are higher in the UK than in other comparable EU countries for some treatable conditions like pneumonia and some cancers. The increase in waiting time means that many people's health care needs are left unmet despite the service being open to everyone and free-at-point-of-use. The UK had less than three doctors for every 1,000 people, and approximately eight nurses for every 1,000 people. Compare that to Germany, where healthcare spending is almost double per person than in Britain, they have almost twice as many doctors and nurses per 100 people. Because the UK has previously relied on European and overseas labour to support the NHS, the post-Brexit position of the service is insecure. The NHS approaching 75 is perhaps not the NHS Nye Bevan dreamed of back in the 1940s.

The WHO report clearly links socioeconomic status with healthcare outcomes, and it would make sense that any overhaul of our NHS services designed to maintain the unique, free-at-point-of-use system we cherish would also include implementation of a UBI. The major debilitating conditions in the UK include asthma, lung cancer, arthritis, dementia, and heart problems. These are conditions that are almost all linked to obesity, smoking and high alcohol consumption – all more prevalent in the lower income groups of British society. In addition, many of the mental health problems currently being offered support by the NHS also have their origins in obesity and lifestyle stress, often the result of financial insecurity and the resulting high state agency involvement in the lives of those affected.

It isn't much of a leap of the imagination to consider that a UBI might also help with NHS staff shortages. In 2019, it was highlighted that there were around 40,000 nursing vacancies, and that the gap would grow with Brexit, not reduce, as it is driven by a shortfall in EU staff. This was partly driven by the austerity measures introduced after 2008, and the need for NHS Trusts to save money. Some of those cost savings were initially found through not replacing nursing posts after employees left. But after a series of concerns were raised over a lack of nursing staff in hospitals, including the Francis Public Inquiry Report into the potentially preventable deaths of 1,200 patients in the care of the Mid Staffordshire

NHS Foundation Trust in 2012, many hospitals realised they needed nurses quickly. These nurses were found from overseas because of a lack of investment in training up UK staff.

However, according to the World Economic Forum the number of people applying to training courses to become a nurse has increased by a third off the back of the pandemic. This is credited to increased public recognition of NHS carers and also perceived job security. A UBI could help boost the numbers of people able to train by opening training up as a viable option for those who otherwise could not afford it. There are many people working in NHS support worker roles who have been unable to study to be a qualified nurse because of the cost. A UBI could also help with job retention by supporting the financial security of those in a profession notoriously underpaid. It could also help balance out the low wages we discussed in the previous chapter.

In the midst of the pandemic, Heath Secretary Matt Hancock undertook a hasty restructure of the way the NHS operates. Central to this was the dissolving of Public Health England (PHE) – created in 2013 to devolve health and wellbeing from central government – and replacing it with the UK Health Security Agency, (initially called the National Institute for Health Protection.) UKHSA became fully operational on 1 October 2021 and combines PHE with the Test and Trace service and the Joint Biosecurity Centre. The move, which sees the focus of healthcare policy shift to pandemic management and future prevention, is not without criticism. Although pandemic communicable diseases post an increasingly valid threat to society in the twenty-first century, in the long term the biggest risk to the health of the UK public appears to be from lifestyle-based diseases which PHE were more focused on, and which a UBI could help with.

Arguably though, if you really want to pandemic-proof a society, then dealing with the financial and social problems that cause insecurity is the best way to insulate your citizens for the future. Supporters of a UBI note that it will give financial freedom to groups who might not otherwise be able to choose safety and security. Victims of domestic violence for example, statistically speaking they are usually women, have increased by 20 per cent globally during the pandemic according to the UN. Trapped at home, heightened tensions, a lack of financial security and the closure of shelters placed an increased number of people in danger. A UBI would allow those potential victims the financial freedom to make positive choices.

A UBI would also mitigate against lost income, reducing the burden of crisis support on government during force majeure events like the pandemic. A UBI also gives workers more control over the conditions of their employment. Some of the true horror stories of the pandemic have related to people working in the back rooms of the online retail industry, placed at risk because they were unable to properly socially distance but were also unable, contractually and financially, to refuse to work. A baseline UBI would allow traditionally low-paid workers to negotiate safer working conditions, better benefits and more competitive pay because they could approach their employer from a place of financial security rather than being at risk.

There have been calls to make UBI the 'NHS' of the twenty-first century. A Universal Basic Income, just like public healthcare, is a leveller. It raises people up, offers them a platform for self-respect and personal development, and as a result it lifts the entirety of society around them. Since the NHS began in 1948, life expectancy has increased by approximately thirteen years, vaccines have turned epidemic diseases into mild seasonal hazards, and the outcome for long-term health problems and disability have markedly improved. But we could do better, and UBI offers us a genuine, respectful and socially responsible pathway to that improvement. It removes the stigma of welfare, and replaces it with entitlement – a baseline standard of living that we all deserve. It offers us a pathway back to our egalitarian evolutionary roots, and the chance to put economy slavery aside in favour of further evolution.

Ultimately, UBI doesn't just offer us the chance to create a new type of NHS, but to save the old one. The healthcare system once loathed by doctors and now beloved; the hallmark of civilised society; the bastion of social equity – it is in crisis, and reversing that crisis isn't just about more funding or yet another restructure. It requires a complete social overhaul, a rewriting of our entire way of thinking about employment, wealth and economics, and thanks to the pandemic we finally have the opportunity to do it – I just hope we take it.

About the Author

Jaime Breitnauer is the author of *The Spanish Flu Epidemic and its Influence on History*, and has worked as a journalist for twenty years. She has a degree and an MA in History and Sociology from the University of Warwick. Breitnauer has a personal interest in how disease has shaped society, and how the shared experience of a pandemic can move humanity closer together, working for shared social good.

Notes

Chapter I

1. Webster, Robert, *Flu Hunter: unlocking the secrets of a virus*, Otago University Press, 2018, p.38
2. ibid, p.40
3. Overton, M, et al, *British Economic Growth, 1300–1850*, 2009. This paper formed part of the project 'Reconstructing the National Income of Britain and Holland, c.1270/1500 to 1850', funded by the Lever Hulme Trust, Reference Number F/00215AR.

Chapter II

1. Ackerknecht, E.H., *A Short History of Medicine*, John Hopkins University Press, 1982, p.81.
2. Kroll, J., & Bachrach, B. (1986) Sin and the Etiology of Disease in Pre-Crusade Europe. Journal of the History of Medicine and Allied Sciences, 41(4), 395-414.
3. Hajar R., The Air of History (Part II) Medicine in the Middle Ages. *Heart Views*. 2012;13(4):158-162. doi:10.4103/1995-705X.105744
4. Krzysztofik M., (2020) The Image of Disease in Religious, Medical-Astrological and Social Discourses: Old Polish Literature as an Example of Early Modern European Mentality. *Journal of religion and health*, 1–10. Advance online publication. https://doi.org/10.1007/s10943-020-01056-x
5. *Baker, John Hamilton (2003)* The Oxford History of the Laws of England: 1483–1558. *Oxford University Press. p.* 97. ISBN 978-0198258179.

Chapter III

1. Norrie, Philip, *A History of Disease in Ancient Times – More Lethal than War*, Palgrave Macmillan, 2016, p.96
2. Robbins Schug, Gwen et al. 'Infection, disease, and biosocial processes at the end of the Indus Civilization.' *PloS one* vol. 8,12 e84814. 17 Dec. 2013, doi:10.1371/journal.pone.0084814
3. Marianna Karamanou, MD, PhD, Gregory Tsoucalas, MD, PhD, Theodore G Papaioannou, PhD, Petros Sfikakis, MD, PhD, Healthcare policy in Ancient Greece: Insights from the Golden Age of Athens (5th century bc) may be useful for medical care in the twenty-first century, *European Heart Journal*, Volume 40, Issue 5, 1 February 2019, Pages 411-412 https://doi.org/10.1093/eurheartj/ehy868
4. Woodhead, A. G. (1952) 'The State Health Service in Ancient Greece.' *Cambridge Historical Journal* 10, no. 3 235-53. http://www.jstor.org/stable/3021113.
5. *Hall, Jonathan M. (2007) A History of the Archaic Greek World: Ca. 1200-479 BCE. John Wiley & Sons. p.129. ISBN 978-0-631-22668-0.*
6. Chiotis, Eustathios & Chioti, Lambrini (2014) Drainage and Sewerage Systems at Ancient Athens, Greece.

Chapter IV

1. R. Rufus Fears, (2004)The Plague Under Marcus Aurelius and the Decline and Fall of the Roman Empire. *Infectious Disease Clinics of North America* 18 (1) : 65. DOI: http://dx.doi.org/10.1016/S0891-5520(03)00089-8
2. C.B. Cunha, B.A. Cunha, (2008) Great Plagues of the Past and Remaining Questions In: D Raoult, M Drancourt, *Paleomicrobiology: Past Human Infections.* Berlin and Heidelberg: Springer-Verlag, pp. 1. DOI: http://dx.doi.org/10.1007/978-3-540-75855-6_1
3. Harbeck M., Seifert L, Hänsch S, Wagner DM, Birdsell D, Parise KL, et al. (2013) *Yersinia pestis* DNA from Skeletal Remains from the sixth century ad Reveals Insights into Justinianic Plague. PLoS Pathog 9(5): e1003349. https://doi.org/10.1371/journal.ppat.1003349
4. E.D. Williamson and P.C.F. Oyston, The natural history and incidence of Yersinia pestis and prospects for vaccination, Journal of Medical Microbiology (2012), 61, 911–918 DOI 10.1099/jmm.0.037960-0
5. McCormick, M. (2003) Rats, Communications, and Plague: Toward an Ecological History. *The Journal of Interdisciplinary History, 34*(1), 1-25. Retrieved May 3, 2021, from http://www.jstor.org/stable/3656705
6. Rosen, W, *Justinian's Flea, Plague, Empire and the Birth of Europe*, Pimlico, 2008, p.215

Chapter V

1. E.A. Webb, 'The founder: To 1123', in *The Records of St. Bartholomew's Priory and St. Bartholomew the Great, West Smithfield: Volume 1* (Oxford, 1921), pp. 37-55. *British History Online* http://www.british-history.ac.uk/st-barts-records/vol1/pp.37-55 [accessed 4 May 2021].
2. Keller., M, et al., Ancient *Yersinia pestis* genomes from across Western Europe reveal early diversification during the First Pandemic (541–750), PNAS June 18, 2019 116 (25) 12363-12372; first published 4 June 2019; https://doi.org/10.1073/pnas.1820447116
3. Katharine R. Dean, Fabienne Krauer, Lars Walløe, Ole Christian Lingjærde, Barbara Bramanti, Nils Chr. Stenseth, and Boris V. Schmid, *Human ectoparasites and the spread of plague in Europe during the Second Pandemic*, PNAS February 6, 2018 115 (6) 1304-1309; first published 16 January 2018; https://doi.org/10.1073/pnas.1715640115

Chapter VI

1. Morens, David M et al. 'Eyewitness accounts of the 1510 influenza pandemic in Europe.' *Lancet* (London, England) vol. 376,9756 (2010): 1894–5. doi:10.1016/s0140-6736(10)62204-0
2. Killingray, David, and Phillips, Howard (eds), (2003), *The Spanish Influenza Pandemic of 1918 to 1919: New Perspectives*, p.138, Routledge
3. Chowell G., Bettencourt L.M., Johnson, N., Alonso, W.J., Viboud C., (2007), 'The 1918–1919 influenza pandemic in England and Wales: spatial patterns in transmissibility and mortality impact'. *Proceedings Biological Sciences*, vol 275 (1634), p.501-9.
4. https://navigator.health.org.uk/theme/ministry-health-act-1919

Chapter VII

1. Nyebevan.com
2. Feeble-Minded Persons (Control) Bill, Hansard, 17 May 1912 vol 38 cc1443-519
3. https://blogs.lse.ac.uk/politicsandpolicy/why-should-the-people-wait-any-longer-how-labour-built-thenhs
4. Beveridge Report on Voluntary Action. (1949) *Monthly Labour Review, 68*(4), 427-429. Retrieved April 26, 2021, from http://www.jstor.org/stable/41831774

Chapter VIII

1. Riedel S. Edward Jenner and the history of smallpox and vaccination. *Proc (Bayl Univ Med Cent)* 2005;18(1):21-25. doi:10.1080/08998280.2005.11928028
2. ibid
3. Millward G. Vaccinating Britain: Mass vaccination and the public since the Second World War [Internet]. Manchester (UK): Manchester University Press; 2019. Chapter 2, Smallpox. Available from: https://www.ncbi.nlm.nih.gov/books/NBK545991/
4. ibid
5. https://www.washingtonpost.com/archive/lifestyle/wellness/1993/02/23/louis-pasteur-and-questions-of-fraud/196b2287-f63f-4bac-874e-c33b122d6f61/
6. https://www.newstatesman.com/world/europe/2020/04/how-polio-outbreak-led-invention-modern-intensive-care#:~:text=In%201952%2C%20an%20epidemic%20of,under%20the%20age%20of%20five.
7. Millward G. Vaccinating Britain: Mass vaccination and the public since the Second World War [Internet]. Manchester (UK): Manchester University Press; 2019. Chapter 3, Poliomyelitis. Available from: https://www.ncbi.nlm.nih.gov/books/NBK545991/
8. ibid
9. Jegede AS. What led to the Nigerian boycott of the polio vaccination campaign? *PLoS Med*. 2007;4(3):e73. doi:10.1371/journal.pmed.0040073
10. Razai M S, Osama T, McKechnie D G J, Majeed A. Covid-19 vaccine hesitancy among ethnic minority groups *BMJ* 2021; 372 :n513 doi:10.1136/bmj.n513

Chapter IX

1. Minghuan Wang,Prof Shabei Xu,Wenhua Liu,Chenyan Zhang,Xiaoxiang Zhang,Liang Wang,Jian Liu,Zhou Zhu,Jianping Hu,Prof Xiang Luo,Prof Wei Wang, Prevalence and changes of BMI categories in China and related chronic diseases: Cross-sectional National Health Service Surveys (NHSSs) from 2013 to 2018, EClinicalMedicine (The Lancet) 11 September 2020, doi 10.1016/j.eclinm.2020.100521
2. Li Y, Teng D, Shi X, Qin Y, Quan H et al. Prevalence of diabetes recorded in mainland China using 2018 diagnostic criteria from the American Diabetes Association: national cross sectional study, *BMJ* 2020; 369:997 doi:10.1136/bmj.m997
3. Blair, Jenny, A Problem in Paradise, Yale Public Health Magazine, January 10th 2018
4. Booth, Helen. P, Charlton, Judith, Gulliford, Martin C., Socioeconomic inequality in morbid obesity with body mass index more than 40kg/m2 in the United States and England, SSM – Population Health, Volume 3, 2017, pp.172-178,
5. Mayor S. Socioeconomic disadvantage is linked to obesity across generations, UK study finds. *BMJ*. 2017 Jan 10;356:j163. doi: 10.1136/bmj.j163. PMID: 28077364.

Chapter X

1. Sharp, Paul M, and Beatrice H Hahn. 'Origins of HIV and the AIDS pandemic.' *Cold Spring Harbor perspectives in medicine* vol. 1,1 (2011): a006841. doi:10.1101/cshperspect.a006841

2. ibid.

3. https://www.independent.co.uk/life-style/health-and-families/health-news/hiv-thirty-years-after-first-diagnosis-britain-heads-100-000-cases-2293194.html

4. Ross J.D., Scott G.R., The association between HIV media campaigns and number of patients coming forward for HIV antibody testing. Genitourin Med. 1993 Jun;69(3):193-5. doi: 10.1136/sti.69.3.193. PMID: 8335311; PMCID: PMC1195061.

5. Beck E.J., Donegan C., Kenny C., Cohen C.S., Moss V, Terry P., Underhill G.S., Jeffries D.J., Pinching A.J., Miller D.L., et al. An update on HIV-testing at a London sexually transmitted diseases clinic: long-term impact of the AIDS media campaigns. Genitourin Med. 1990 Jun;66(3):142-7. doi: 10.1136/sti.66.3.142. PMID: 2370058; PMCID: PMC1194492.

6. Fingleton, NiamhA, C MargaretWatson, and Catriona Matheson. 'You are still a human being, you still have needs, you still have wants': a qualitative exploration of patients' experiences and views of HIV support.' Journal of Public Health 40.4 (2018)

Chapter XI

1. Harper D.R., Preparedness for SARS in the UK in 2003. Philos Trans R Soc Lond B Biol Sci. 2004 Jul 29;359(1447):1131-2. doi: 10.1098/rstb.2004.1485. PMID: 15306400; PMCID: PMC1693396.

2. Goddard, N L et al. 'Lessons learned from SARS: the experience of the Health Protection Agency, England.' *Public health* vol. 120,1 (2006): 27-32. doi:10.1016/j.puhe.2005.10.003

3. Roos, R, Study puts global 2009 H1N1 infection rate at 11% to 21%, CIDRAP, August 2011.

4. Mahase E. Covid-19: Was the decision to delay the UK's lockdown over fears of 'behavioural fatigue' based on evidence? *BMJ* 2020; 370 :m3166 doi:10.1136/bmj.m3166

5. https://blogs.bmj.com/bmj/2021/01/29/up-the-line-to-death-covid-19-has-revealed-a-mortal-betrayal-of-the-worlds-healthcare-workers/

Chapter XII

1. Marlowe, F. (2005) Hunter-gatherers and human evolution. Evolutionary Anthropology, 14(2), 54-67.

2. https://www.resilience.org/stories/2020-09-04/basic-income-could-virtually-eliminate-poverty-in-the-united-kingdom-at-a-cost-of-67-billion-per-year/?fbclid=IwAR2qSHP_R27YRMOVap_cxDsr4hQR_kiRe9GArY0gy9391nWjobB8T00i9UY#:~:text=The%20cost%20of%20a%20full,and%20%C2%A33%2C853%20for%20children.&text=This%20UBI%20system%20eliminates%20absolute,United%20States

3. Patel S.B., Kariel J., Universal Basic Income and Covid-19 pandemic *BMJ* 2021; 372 :n193 doi:10.1136/bmj.n193

4. https://www.euro.who.int/__data/assets/pdf_file/0006/419478/Country-Health-Profile-2019-United-Kingdom.pdf

Bibliography

Books

Ackerknecht, E.H., *A Short History of Medicine*, John Hopkins University Press, (1982)

Almeroth-Williams, Thomas, *City of Beasts: How Animals Shaped Georgian London*, Manchester University Press, (2019)

Arnold, Catherine, *Pandemic 1918: The story of the deadliest influenza in history*, Michael O'Mara Books Ltd, (2018)

Baker, John Hamilton (2003). The Oxford History of the Laws of England: 1483–1558. Oxford University Press

Bevan, Aneurin, In Place of Fear, Quartet, (1952)

Breitnauer, Jaime, *The Spanish Flu Pandemic and its Influence on History*, Pen and Sword, (2019)

Cartledge, Paul, *The Spartans: An Epic History*, Pan Books, (2002)

Collier, R, *The plague of the Spanish Lady*, MacMillan, (1974)

Cohn, Jr., Samuel K, *Epidemics: Hate and Compassion from the Plague of Athens to AIDs*, Oxford University Press, (2018)

Greenblatt, Stephen, *The Swerve: How the Renaissance Began*, Bodley Head, (2011)

Hall, Edith, *Introducing the Ancient Greeks*, Bodley Head, (2015)

Jenkinson, Dr Andrew, *Why We Eat (Too Much) – the new science of appetite*, Penguin, (2020)

Joint Association of Classical Teachers', *The World of Athens*, Cambridge University Press, (1984)

Killingray, David, and Phillips, Howard (eds), *The Spanish Influenza Pandemic of 1918 to 1919: New Perspectives*, Routledge (2003)

Lacy, Robert, *Great Tales from English History*, Little Brown, (2003)

Lee, Christopher, *This Sceptred Isle: The making of the British*, Constable (2012)

Le Goff, Jacques, *The Birth of Europe*, Blackwell (2005)

Miller, Timothy, *The Birth of the Hospital in the Byzantine Empire*, John Hopkins University Press (1985)

Millward G., *Vaccinating Britain: Mass vaccination and the public since the Second World War* [Internet]. Manchester (UK): Manchester University Press (2019) https://www.ncbi.nlm.nih.gov/books/NBK545991/

Norris, Philip, *A History of Disease in Ancient Times – More Lethal than War*, Palgrave Macmillan (2016)

Rice, Geoffrey, *Black November: The 1918 influenza pandemic in New Zealand*, Canterbury University Press (2016)

Rivett, Geoffrey, *From Cradle to Grave: Fifty Years of the NHS*, Kings Fund (1998)

Robbins Schug, Gwen et al. 'Infection, disease, and biosocial processes at the end of the Indus Civilization.' *PloS one* vol. 8,12 e84814. 17 Dec. 2013, doi:10.1371/journal.pone.0084814

Rosen, W., *Justinian's Flea, Plague, Empire and the Birth of Europe*, Pimlico (2008)

Spiker, P., *Social Policy Theory and Practice*, Policy Press (2014)

Spivey, Nigel, *Classical Civilization: Greeks and Romans in 10 Chapters*, Head of Zeus (2015)

Spinney, Laura, *Pale Rider: The Spanish flu of 1918 and how it changed the world*, Vintage, (2017)

Webster, Robert, *Flu Hunter: unlocking the secrets of a virus*, Otago University Press (2018)

Websites

https://www.ucl.ac.uk/~ucgajpd/medicina%20antiqua/sa_hippint.html

https://www.thecollector.com/sparta-fearless-warriors/

https://www.theatlantic.com/science/archive/2016/02/what-made-ancient-athens-a-city-of-genius/462009/

https://www.nationalgeographic.com/foodfeatures/evolution-of-diet/

https://www.theguardian.com/science/2016/aug/24/how-did-the-chicken-a-shy-forest-bird-migrate-around-the-globe-new-zealan

https://www.otago.ac.nz/alumni/news/robert-webster.html

https://www.smithsonianmag.com/science-nature/the-flu-hunter-107190623/

https://navigator.health.org.uk/theme/ministry-health-act-1919

https://www.cam.ac.uk/research/features/healthy-vs-unhealthy-food-the-challenges-of-understanding-food-choices

https://www.bbc.co.uk/news/health-43504125

https://www.longtermplan.nhs.uk/online-version/chapter-2-more-nhs-action-on-prevention-and-health-inequalities/obesity/

https://www.nutritioninsight.com/news/junk-food-ad-spending-outstrips-uk-government-campaigns-as-healthcare-costs-of-obesity-soar.html#:~:text=The%20UK%20government%20spent%20%C2%A3,%C2%A35.1%20billion%20a%20year.

https://sciencenordic.com/denmark-obesity-society--culture/19th-century-undertaker-introduced-the-world-to-dieting/1436238

https://theconversation.com/what-the-archaeological-record-reveals-about-epidemics-throughout-history-and-the-human-response-to-them-138408

https://www.sciencemag.org/news/2020/09/leprosy-covid-19-how-stigma-makes-it-harder-fight-epidemics

https://slate.com/technology/2014/08/ebola-is-not-gods-wrath-religious-leaders-say-disease-is-caused-by-sin-and-cured-by-god.html

www.Nyebevan.com

https://blogs.lse.ac.uk/politicsandpolicy/why-should-the-people-wait-any-longer-how-labour-built-thenhs

https://www.gponline.com/nhs-70-general-practice-1948-1967/article/1485294

https://blogs.lse.ac.uk/politicsandpolicy/why-should-the-people-wait-any-longer-how-labour-built-the-nhs

https://www.theguardian.com/commentisfree/2012/dec/07/william-beveridge-hated-term-welfare-state

https://www.theguardian.com/society/2017/oct/10/beveridge-five-evils-welfare-state

https://www.theguardian.com/commentisfree/2012/feb/17/eugenics-skeleton-rattles-loudest-closet-left

https://www.newstatesman.com/society/2010/12/british-eugenics-disabled

https://www.independent.co.uk/life-style/health-and-families/health-news/hiv-thirty-years-after-first-diagnosis-britain-heads-100-000-cases-2293194.html
https://www.walesonline.co.uk/news/wales-news/newport-hiv-its-a-sin-19752900
www.tht.org.uk
https://level.medium.com/how-it-feels-to-live-with-aids-for-30-years-ae7b8f614b62
https://placingthepublic.lshtm.ac.uk/2018/05/20/remembering-the-dont-die-of-ignorance-campaign/
https://time.com/4705809/first-aids-drug-azt/
https://www.theguardian.com/commentisfree/2018/sep/27/nhs-fund-anti-hiv-drugs-prep
https://blogs.bmj.com/bmj/2021/01/29/up-the-line-to-death-covid-19-has-revealed-a-mortal-betrayal-of-the-worlds-healthcare-workers/
https://www.nursingtimes.net/news/coronavirus/clap-for-heroes-nurses-say-they-do-not-want-return-of-applause-07-01-2021/
https://www.theguardian.com/world/2020/jun/10/uk-coronavirus-lockdown-20000-lives-boris-johnson-neil-ferguson
https://www.telegraph.co.uk/global-health/science-and-disease/six-crucial-pandemic-lessons-government-ignored/
https://www.nytimes.com/2007/10/11/world/africa/11polio.html
https://www.virology.ws/2015/09/10/why-do-we-still-use-sabin-poliovirus-vaccine/
https://www.washingtonpost.com/archive/lifestyle/wellness/1993/02/23/louis-pasteur-and-questions-of-fraud/196b2287-f63f-4bac-874e-c33b122d6f61/
https://www.newstatesman.com/world/europe/2020/04/how-polio-outbreak-led-invention-modern-intensive-care#:~:text=In%201952%2C%20an%20epidemic%20of,under%20the%20age%20of%20five.
https://theconversation.com/the-deadly-polio-epidemic-and-why-it-matters-for-coronavirus-133976
https://www.nature.com/articles/d41586-020-01019-y
https://janetparker.birminghamlive.co.uk/#a-lonely-death-PHDlW52yaV
https://www.resilience.org/stories/2020-09-04/basic-income-could-virtually-eliminate-poverty-in-the-united-kingdom-at-a-cost-of-67-billion-per-year

Podcasts
Futuremakers: A History of Pandemics, University of Oxford
A History of Pandemics, University of Belfast

Periodicals and articles
Anderson, G., (1963). Medieval Medicine for Sin. *Journal of Religion and Health*, 2(2), 156-165. Retrieved 23 April 2021, from http://www.jstor.org/stable/27504551
Baicus, A., History of polio vaccination. *World J Virol*. 2012;1(4):108-114. doi:10.5501/wjv.v1.i4.108
Barberis, I., Myles P., Ault S.K., Bragazzi N.L., Martini M., History and evolution of influenza control through vaccination: from the first monovalent vaccine to universal vaccines. *J Prev Med Hyg*. 2016;57(3):E115-E120.
Beck, E.J., Donegan C., Kenny C., Cohen C.S., Moss V., Terry P., Underhill G.S., Jeffries D.J., Pinching A.J., Miller D.L., et al. An update on HIV-testing at a London sexually transmitted diseases clinic: long-term impact of the AIDS media campaigns. Genitourin Med. 1990 Jun;66(3):142-7. doi: 10.1136/sti.66.3.142. PMID: 2370058; PMCID: PMC1194492.

Beveridge Report on Voluntary Action. (1949). *Monthly Labor Review, 68*(4), 427-429. Retrieved April 26, 2021, from http://www.jstor.org/stable/41831774

Blair, Jenny, 'A Problem in Paradise', *Yale Public Health Magazine*, 10 January 2018

Broushaki, Farnaz et al, Early Neolithic genomes from the eastern Fertile Crescent, *Science*, Vol 353, is 6298, 29 July 2016, p499–503

Booth, Helen P., Charlton, Judith, Gulliford, Martin C., Socioeconomic inequality in morbid obesity with body mass index more than 40kg/m2 in the United States and England, SSM – Population Health, Volume 3, 2017, Pages 172-178.

Chang A., Schulz P., Tu S., Liu M., Communicative Blame in Online Communication of the COVID-19 Pandemic: Computational Approach of Stigmatizing Cues and Negative Sentiment Gauged With Automated Analytic Techniques, J Med Internet Res 2020;22(11):e21504
URL: https://www.jmir.org/2020/11/e21504, DOI: 10.2196/21504

Chiotis, Eustathios & Chioti, Lambrini (2014) Drainage and Sewerage Systems at Ancient Athens, Greece.

Christaki, Eirini. 'New technologies in predicting, preventing and controlling emerging infectious diseases.' *Virulence* vol. 6,6 (2015): 558-65. doi:10.1080/21505594.2015.1040975

Chomel, B.B.. 'Zoonoses.' *Encyclopedia of Microbiology* (2009): 820–829. doi:10.1016/B978-012373944-5.00213-3

Chowell G., Bettencourt L.M., Johnson, N., Alonso, W.J., Vibound C., (2007), 'The 1918-1919 influenza pandemic in England and Wales: spatial patterns in transmissibility and mortality impact'. *Proceedings Biological Sciences*, vol 275 (1634), p.501-9.

C.B. Cunha, B.A. Cunha, (2008). Great Plagues of the Past and Remaining Questions In: D. Raoult, M. Drancourt, *Paleomicrobiology: Past Human Infections*. Berlin and Heidelberg: Springer-Verlag, pp. 1. DOI: http://dx.doi.org/10.1007/978-3-540-75855-6_1

Katharine R. Dean, Fabienne Krauer, Lars Walløe, Ole Christian Lingjærde, Barbara Bramanti, Nils Chr. Stenseth, and Boris V. Schmid, *Human ectoparasites and the spread of plague in Europe during the Second Pandemic*, PNAS 6 February 2018 115 (6) 1304-1309; first published 16 January 2018; https://doi.org/10.1073/pnas.1715640115

Fingleton, Niamh A., C. Margaret Watson, and Catriona Matheson. '"You are still a human being, you still have needs, you still have wants": a qualitative exploration of patients' experiences and views of HIV support.' Journal of Public Health 40.4 (2018).

Goddard, N.L. et al. 'Lessons learned from SARS: the experience of the Health Protection Agency, England.' *Public health* vol. 120,1 (2006): 27-32. doi:10.1016/j.puhe.2005.10.003

Gorsky M.. The NHS in Britain: Any Lesson from History for Universal Health Coverage? In: Medcalf A., Bhattacharya S., Momen H., et al., (eds) Health For All: The Journey of Universal Health Coverage. Hyderabad (IN): Orient Blackswan; 2015. Chapter 7. Available from: https://www.ncbi.nlm.nih.gov/books/NBK316274/

Hall, Jonathan M., *A History of the Archaic Greek World: Ca. 1200-479 bce*, John Wiley & Sons (2007)

Harbeck M., Seifert L., Hänsch S., Wagner D.M., Birdsell D., Parise K.L., et al. (2013) *Yersinia pestis* DNA from Skeletal Remains from the 6th Century ad Reveals Insights into Justinianic Plague. PLoS Pathog 9(5): e1003349. https://doi.org/10.1371/journal.ppat.1003349

Harper DR. Preparedness for SARS in the UK in 2003. Philos Trans R Soc Lond B Biol Sci. 2004 Jul 29;359(1447):1131-2. doi: 10.1098/rstb.2004.1485. PMID: 15306400; PMCID: PMC1693396.

Hajar R. The Air of History (Part II) Medicine in the Middle Ages. *Heart Views*. 2012;13(4):158-162. doi:10.4103/1995-705X.105744

Holladay, A. J., and J.C.F. Poole. Thucydides and the Plague of Athens, *The Classical Quarterly*, vol. 29, no. 2, 1979, pp. 282–300. *JSTOR*, www.jstor.org/stable/638096. Accessed 13 March 2021.

Jegede A.S., What led to the Nigerian boycott of the polio vaccination campaign?. *PLoS Med*. 2007;4(3):e73. doi:10.1371/journal.pmed.0040073

Jefferys, K. (1987) British Politics and Social Policy during the Second World War. *The Historical Journal, 30*(1), 123-144. Retrieved 27 April 2021, from http://www.jstor. org/stable/2639308

Kannadan, Ajesh (2018) 'History of the Miasma Theory of Disease,' ESSAI: Vol. 16, Article 18. Available at: https://dc.cod.edu/essai/vol16/iss1/18

Karesh, William B, et al, 'Ecology of Zoonoses: Natural and unnatural histories', The Lancet, Vol 380, issue 9857, December 1st, 2012, p1936-1945

Karamanou, Marianna MD, PhD, Tsoucalas, Gregory MD, PhD, Papaioannou, Theodore G. PhD, Sfikakis, Petros MD, PhD, Healthcare policy in Ancient Greece: Insights from the Golden Age of Athens (5th century bc) may be useful for medical care in the 21st century, *European Heart Journal*, Volume 40, Issue 5, 1 February 2019, Pages 411–412, https://doi.org/10.1093/eurheartj/ehy868

Keller, M., et al., Ancient *Yersinia pestis* genomes from across Western Europe reveal early diversification during the First Pandemic (541–750), PNAS 18 June 2019 116 (25) 12363-12372; first published 4 June 2019; https://doi.org/10.1073/pnas.1820447116

Khubchandani, Jagdish et al. 'Ebola, Zika, Corona…What Is Next for Our World?' *International journal of environmental research and public health* vol. 17,9 3171. 2 May. 2020, doi:10.3390/ijerph17093171

Klatt, Nichole R., et al. 'Nonpathogenic simian immunodeficiency virus infections.' *Cold Spring Harbor perspectives in medicine* vol. 2,1 (2012): a007153. doi:10.1101/cshperspect.a007153

Kleisiaris, Christos F. et al. Health care practices in ancient Greece: The Hippocratic ideal.' *Journal of medical ethics and history of medicine* vol. 7 6. 15 Mar. 2014

Kroll, J., & Bachrach, B., (1986) Sin and the Etiology of Disease in Pre-Crusade Europe. Journal of the History of Medicine and Allied Sciences, 41(4), 395-414.

Krzysztofik M., (2020) The Image of Disease in Religious, Medical-Astrological and Social Discourses: Old Polish Literature as an Example of Early Modern European Mentality. *Journal of religion and health*, 1–10. Advance online publication. https://doi.org/10.1007/s10943-020-01056-x

LeDuc, James W., and M,. Anita Barry, 'SARS, the First Pandemic of the 21st Century.' *Emerging Infectious Diseases* vol. 10,11 (2004): e26. doi:10.3201/eid1011.040797_02

Li Y, Teng D, Shi X, Qin Y, Quan H et al. Prevalence of diabetes recorded in mainland China using 2018 diagnostic criteria from the American Diabetes Association: national cross sectional study, BMJ 2020; 369:997 doi:10.1136/bmj.m997

Mahase E., Covid-19: Was the decision to delay the UK's lockdown over fears of 'behavioural fatigue' based on evidence? *BMJ* 2020; 370 :m3166 doi:10.1136/bmj.m3166

Martin, Paul M.V. and Martin-Granel, Estelle, 2,500-year Evolution of the Term Pandemic, *Journal of Emerging Infectious Diseases*, Vol 12, issue 6, June 2006, pages 976-980

McCormick, M. (2003) Rats, Communications, and Plague: Toward an Ecological History. *The Journal of Interdisciplinary History, 34*(1), 1-25. Retrieved 3 May 2021, from http://www.jstor.org/stable/3656705

Marlowe, F., (2005) Hunter-gatherers and human evolution. Evolutionary Anthropology, 14(2), 54-67.

https://www.euro.who.int/__data/assets/pdf_file/0006/419478/Country-Health-Profile-2019-United-Kingdom.pdf

Mayor S., Socioeconomic disadvantage is linked to obesity across generations, UK study finds. *BMJ*. 10 January 2017; 356:j163. doi: 10.1136/bmj.j163. PMID: 28077364.

McMichael, Tony. 'Twenty-First Century Plague. The Story of SARS.' *Social history of medicine: the journal of the Society for the Social History of Medicine* vol. 18,3 (2005): 495-496. doi:10.1093/shm/hki053

Mitchell N.S., Catenacci V.A., Wyatt H.R., Hill J.O., Obesity: overview of an epidemic. *Psychiatr Clin North Am*. 2011;34(4):717-732. doi:10.1016/j.psc.2011.08.005

Minghuan Wang, Prof Shabei Xu, Wenhua Liu, Chenyan Zhang, Xiaoxiang Zhang, Liang Wang, Jian Liu, Zhou Zhu, Jianping Hu, Prof Xiang Luo, Prof Wei Wang, Prevalence and changes of BMI categories in China and related chronic diseases: Cross-sectional National Health Service Surveys (NHSSs) from 2013 to 2018, EClinicalMedicine (*The Lancet*) 11 September 2020, doi 10.1016/j.eclinm.2020.100521

Milner, George R., Early agriculture's toll on human health, *Proceedings of the National Academy of Sciences* July 2019, 116 (28) 13721-13723; DOI: 10.1073/pnas.1908960116

Morens, David M et al. 'Eyewitness accounts of the 1510 influenza pandemic in Europe.' *Lancet (London, England)* vol. 376,9756 (2010): 1894-5. doi:10.1016/s0140-6736(10)62204-0

Murray, Jillian, and Adam L. Cohen. 'Infectious Disease Surveillance.' *International Encyclopedia of Public Health* (2017): 222–229. doi:10.1016/B978-0-12-803678-5.00517-8

Overton, M., et al, *British Economic Growth, 1300–1850*, 2009. This paper formed part of the project 'Reconstructing the National Income of Britain and Holland, c.1270/1500 to 1850', funded by the Lever Hulme Trust, Reference Number F/00215AR.

Patel S.B. Kariel J., Universal Basic Income and Covid-19 pandemic *BMJ* 2021; 372 :n193 doi:10.1136/bmj.n193

Peate, I. (2016). NHS England's HIV scandal, *British Journal of Nursing*, 25(17), 947-947.

Pinault, Jody Rubin, How Hippocrates Cured the Plague, *Journal of the History of Medicine and Allied Sciences*, Volume 41, Issue 1, January 1986, Pages 52–75, https://doi.org/10.1093/jhmas/41.1.52

Ross J.D., Scott G.R., The association between HIV media campaigns and number of patients coming forward for HIV antibody testing. Genitourin Med. 1993 Jun;69(3):193-5. doi: 10.1136/sti.69.3.193. PMID: 8335311; PMCID: PMC1195061

Roos, R, Study puts global 2009 H1N1 infection rate at 11% to 21%, CIDRAP, August 2011.

Riedel S., Edward Jenner and the history of smallpox and vaccination. *Proc (Bayl Univ Med Cent)*. 2005;18(1):21-25. doi:10.1080/08998280.2005.11928028

Razai M.S., Osama T, McKechnie D.G.J., Majeed A., Covid-19 vaccine hesitancy among ethnic minority groups *BMJ* 2021; 372 :n513 doi:10.1136/bmj.n513

R Rufus Fears, (2004) The Plague Under Marcus Aurelius and the Decline and Fall of the Roman Empire. *Infectious Disease Clinics of North America* 18 (1) : 65. DOI: http://dx.doi.org/10.1016/S0891-5520(03)00089-8

Sampson, C., O'Neill, P. and Lorgelly, P., The Impact of New Medicines in the NHS; 70 Years of Innovation, Office of Health Economics, August 2018.

Sharp, Paul M., and Beatrice H Hahn. 'Origins of HIV and the AIDS pandemic.' *Cold Spring Harbor perspectives in medicine* vol. 1,1 (2011): a006841. doi:10.1101/cshperspect.a006841

Shimizu K., 'History of influenza epidemics and discovery of influenza virus'. Nihon Rinsho. 1997 Oct;55(10):2505-11. Japanese. PMID: 9360364.

Sabbatani S., Fiorino S. La peste antonina e il declino dell'Impero Romano. Ruolo della guerra partica e della guerra marcomannica tra il 164 e il 182 d.c. nella diffusione del contagio 'The Antonine Plague and the decline of the Roman Empire'. Infez Med. 2009 Dec;17(4):261-75. Italian. PMID: 20046111.

Vigarello, Georges, and C. Jon Delogu, *The Metamorphoses of Fat: A History of Obesity*. Columbia University Press, 2013. *JSTOR*, www.jstor.org/stable/10.7312/viga15976. Accessed 13 Apr. 2021.

Virtual Mentor. 2006;8(4):219-222. doi: 10.1001/virtualmentor.2006.8.4.jdsc1-0604.

Williamson, E.D. and P.C.F. Oyston, The natural history and incidence of Yersinia pestis and prospects for vaccination, *Journal of Medical Microbiology* (2012), 61, 911–918 DOI 10.1099/jmm.0.037960-0

Webb, E.A., 'The founder: To 1123', in *The Records of St. Bartholomew's Priory and St. Bartholomew the Great, West Smithfield: Volume 1* (Oxford, 1921), pp. 37-55. *British History Online* http://www.british-history.ac.uk/st-barts-records/vol1/pp37-55 [accessed 4 May 2021].

Worobey M., Gemmel M., Teuwen D.E., Haselkorn T., Kunstman K., Bunce M., Muyembe J.J., Kabongo .JM., Kalengayi R.M., Van Marck E., Gilbert M.T., Wolinsky S.M,. Direct evidence of extensive diversity of HIV-1 in Kinshasa by 1960. Nature. 2008 Oct 2;455(7213):661-4. doi: 10.1038/nature07390. PMID: 18833279; PMCID: PMC3682493.

Woodhead, A.G., (1952). 'The State Health Service in Ancient Greece.' *Cambridge Historical Journal* 10, no. 3 235-53. http://www.jstor.org/stable/3021113.

Zhou L, Cao D, Si Y, et al ,'Income-related inequities of adult obesity and central obesity in China: evidence from the China Health and Nutrition Survey 1997–2011' *BMJ Open* 2020;**10**:e034288. doi: 10.1136/bmjopen-2019-034288

Feeble-Minded Persons (Control) Bill, Hansard, 17 May 1912 vol 38 cc1443-519